T0359426

PUBLISHED BY BOOM BOOKS

www.boombooks.biz

ABOUT THIS BOOK

I was born in 1934, so that I can remember well a great deal of what went on around me from 1939 onwards. But of course, the bulk of this book's material came from research. That meant that I spent many hours in front of a computer reading electronic versions of newspapers, magazines, Hansard, Ministers' Press releases and the like. My task was to sift out, day-by-day, those stories and events that would be of interest to the most readers.

Then I supplemented these with materials from books, broadcasts, memoirs, biographies, government reports and statistics. And I talked to old-timers, one-on-one, and in organised groups, and to Baby Boomers about their recollections. People with stories to tell came out of the woodwork, and talked about the tragic, and funny, and commonplace events that have shaped their lives.

I think I have covered most of the major issues that people then were interested in. On the other hand, in some cases I have dwelt a little on minor frivolous matters, perhaps to the detriment of more sober considerations. Still, in the long run, this makes the book more readable, and hopefully it will convey adequately the spirit of the times.

Overall, I expect I can make you wonder, remember, rage and giggle, and I hope that you and your family will find some comfort in the realisation that no matter how new and novel a current situation is to you, it has all happened often before.

BORN IN 1950?

WHAT ELSE HAPPENED?

RON WILLIAMS

AUSTRALIAN SOCIAL HISTORY

BOOK 12 IN A SERIES OF 35
FROM 1939 to 1973

War Babies Years (1939 to 1945):   7 Titles
Baby Boom Years (1946 to 1960):   15 Titles
Post Boom Years (1961 to 1972):   13 Titles

BOOM, BOOM BABY, BOOM

BORN IN 1950? WHAT ELSE HAPPENED?

Published by Boom Books. Wickham, NSW, Australia
Web: boombooks.biz
Email: jen@boombooks.biz

© Ron Williams 2013. This revised edition: 2023

A single chapter or part thereof may be copied and
reproduced without permission, provided that the
Author, Title, and Web Site are acknowledged.

Title: Born in 1950? What else happened?
Ron Williams
ISBN: 9780648651192

Cover image: National Archives of Australia.
A462, 778 03 PART 2, Prime Minister Ben Chifley;
A1200, L13020, Policewoman and bus;
A1200, L13454, mob of sheep;
Mitchell Library, a1176301, Darcy Dugan mug shot.

CONTENTS

SOME IMPORTANT PEOPLE AND EVENTS

King of England	George VI
Prime Minister of Oz	Robert Menzies
Leader of Opposition	Dr H Evatt
Governor General	William McKell
The Pope	Pius XII
US President	Harry Truman
PM of Britain	Clement Atlee

Winner of the Ashes:

1948	Australia 4 - 0
1950 - 51	Australia 4 -1
1953	England 1 - 0

Melbourne Cup Winners:

1949	Foxzami
1950	Comic Court
1951	Delta

Academy Awards:

Best Actor	Jose Ferrer
Best Actress	Judy Holliday
Best Movie	All About Eve

PREFACE TO THIS SERIES: 1939 to 1973

This book is the 12th in **a series** of books that I have researched and written. It tells a story about a number of important or newsworthy Australia-centric events that happened in 1950 **The series** covers each of the years from 1939 to 1973, for a total of 35 books.

I developed my interest in writing these books a few years ago at a time when my children entered their teens. My own teens started in 1947, and I started trying to remember what had happened to me then. I thought of the big events first, like Saturday afternoon at the pictures, and cricket in the back yard, and the wonderful fun of going to Maitland on the train for school each day. Then I recalled some of the not-so-good things. I was an altar boy, and that meant three or four Masses a week. I might have thought I loved God at that stage, but I really hated his Masses. And the schoolboy bullies, like Greg Barrell, and the hapless Freddie Evatt. Yet, to compensate for these, there was always the beautiful, black headed, blue-sailor-suited June Browne, who I was allowed to worship from a distance.

I also thought about my parents. Most of the major events that I lived through came to mind readily. But after that, I realised that I really knew very little about these parents of mine. They had been born about the start of the Twentieth Century, and they died in 1970 and 1980. For their last 20 years, I was old enough to speak with a bit of sense. I could have talked to them a lot about their lives. I could have found out about the times they lived in. But I did not. I know almost nothing about them really. Their courtship? Working in the pits? The Lock-out in the Depression?

Losing their second child? Being dusted as a miner? The shootings at Rothbury? My uncles killed in the War? There were hundreds, thousands of questions that I would now like to ask them. But, alas, I can't. It's too late.

Thus, prompted by my guilt, I resolved to write these books. They describe happenings that affected people, real people. In **1950,** there is some coverage of international affairs, but a lot more on social events within Australia. This book, and the whole series is, to coin a modern phrase, designed to push the reader's buttons, to make you remember and wonder at things forgotten. The books might just let nostalgia see the light of day, so that oldies and youngies will talk about the past and re-discover a heritage otherwise forgotten. Hopefully, they will spark discussions between generations, and foster the asking and the answering of questions that should not remain unanswered.

The sources of my material. I was born in 1934, so that I can remember well a great deal of what went on around me from 1939 onwards. But of course, the bulk of this book's material came from research. That meant that I spent many hours in front of a computer reading electronic versions of newspapers, like the *Sydney Morning Herald (SMH)*, magazines, Hansard, Ministers' Press releases and the like. My task was to sift out, **day-by-day**, those stories and events that would be of interest to most readers. Then I supplemented these with materials from books, broadcasts, memoirs, biographies, government reports and statistics. And I talked to old-timers, one-on-one, and in organised groups, and to Baby Boomers about their recollections. People with stories to tell came out of the woodwork, and talked no end about the tragic, and funny, and commonplace events that have shaped their lives.

The presentation of each book. For each year covered, the end result is a collection of short Chapters on many of the topics that concerned ordinary people in that year. I think I have covered most of the major issues that people then were interested in. On the other hand, in some cases I have dwelt a little on minor frivolous matters, perhaps to the detriment of more sober considerations. Still, in the long run, this makes the book more readable, and hopefully it will convey adequately the spirit of the times.

Each of the books is mainly Sydney based, but I have been **deliberately national in outlook**, so that readers elsewhere will feel comfortable that I am talking about matters that affected them personally. After all, housing shortages and strikes and juvenile delinquency involved **all** Australians, and other issues, such as problems overseas, had no State component in them. Overall, I expect I can make you wonder, remember, rage and giggle equally, no matter where you hail from.

INTRO TO 1950

1950 was well-and-truly a Baby Boom year. The nation's fertility rate had started to increase when the Diggers returned, and about 1948, this higher fertility started to gallop. By 1950, it was still rising, and it left for dead anything that had been seen before the War. On top of that, over 100,000 British and European migrants were coming here every year, so that our population was booming. This meant plenty of jobs, lots of new houses, new cars and Hills Hoists, trips to the bank manager, and all the other signs of prosperity. There was a new political Party in office, and it brought with it ideas that had been pent up for a decade, so it was likely to be a time of action. We'll see.

BACKGROUND FROM 1949

1950 started with all sorts of prominent figures telling us that we were at the beginning of a brand-new half century. It followed from this that we now had the opportunity to move away from our mistakes of the past, to forget all our previous follies, and go forward in a wiser and supposedly happier world. The message from the King, George VI, though full of warning, still dwelt on the splendid opportunities that now presented. The **new** Prime Minister, Bob Menzies, spoke in similar vein, as did heaps of churchmen, Premiers, and newspaper editorials. They were reinforced by identical messages from overseas, where British politicians like Clement Attlee and Winston Churchill were very confident that the British Empire was intact, and that they could happily give sound advice to colonies and dominions that were thousands of miles away from them.

Here in Australia we had a few narks who did their best to spoil this joyous occasion by writing Letters to the newspapers saying that 1950 was **not** the start of a **new half-century, but rather the end of an old one**. After all, they reasoned, if you start counting from 1 to 10, you start at 1 and **finish at 10**. So that meant we should not yet change our ways, and should instead struggle on in our non-reformed state **for another year**. Fortunately, we had many other writers who were quick to respond that there were 50 years in a half-century, and so when we got to 50, that was clearly the end of the old, **and** the start of the new. It was obviously a weighty discussion, and that was why **it monopolised the Letters columns for the first two weeks** of the year.

Of course, the start of this year was not much different from the start of any other, in that **almost everyone was on holidays,** living in tents and shacks up and down the coast, and using their spare energy to play cards and backyard cricket, with the occasional drop of beer to help with the thirst. For the whole month of January, legions of people simply got away from it all, forgot all the crises that always worried them in other months, and turned a blind eye to what little news came their way.

Fortunately, the task of ignoring the news was made much easier by the fact that most employees of newspapers and radio stations had also gone on holidays, and had joined the idle and indolent. Newspapers were half their normal volume, the classified ads were down to almost nothing, and it would have seemed that the hatreds and disputes that had wracked the world a few weeks ago had all gone away. Alas, that was not the case, and when it came to later months, **world troubles were back with a vengeance**.

In the meantime, there was time to ruminate on the changes that were obviously just ahead for the nation. The most obvious was that **a new government had just been elected** in polls that had seen the Labor Party annihilated, and the Liberal-Country Party given the reins. That meant that Ben Chifley was out as Prime Minister, and that Bob Menzies was in. Importantly, it meant that the ideas for **socialisation** that had been Chifley's platform for decades

had been dealt a death-blow, and so-called free enterprise became the catchword of the new rulers.

It also meant, hopefully, that many of **the restrictions on all sorts of goods and services that had persisted since the War** years might now be removed. For example, the nation was still suffering from rationing of petrol and butter, and also from all sorts of controls on rents, and housing and what-have-you. Even the sale of cream was officially forbidden because it was supposedly used to produce the butter that was so badly needed in Britain. Every man and his dog were now hoping that Menzies would live up to his election promises to get rid of a lot of these enforced unnecessary austerities.

The other matter on the immediate Menzies agenda was his determination **to exploit the "Red menace" to the full.** Here, he had **two** different but related tacks. **The first** was that the local Communists had, since the end of the War, gained power in many of the nation's Trade Unions, and had foisted a never-ending series of strikes on the population. Menzies claimed that the Reds were intent on bringing Australia to its knees by crippling industry, and that unless he destroyed their power, they would do just that, and allow the nation to follow the same path as Russia.

The second was that overseas the Communists had already gained power in many countries, often by dubious means, and were on the warpath to gain more conquests. At the start of 1950, the Reds in China had just vanquished the Nationalists, and were so much in control that many governments, including Britain, were about to recognise them as the official government. Menzies feared, he said, that in terms of Australia, **the Domino Theory** was about to materialise. That is, that the Chinese forces would roll down through Indo-China into Malaysia and Singapore, and through Indonesia, and ultimately into Australia, and finally get **its ultimate goal** which was surely Tasmania. Given the anti-Red witch-hunts that were occurring overseas – these were the McCarthy years in America – it was hard to argue against all of this happening. We will return a few times in this book to the *"Reds under the Beds"* theme.

Three other matters from the past. To set the scene for this book, I will briefly outline three situations that have ongoing consequences. The **first** relates to the economy. Let me simply say **the nation was doing very well**. The prices for our commodities were high overseas, everyone had a job, housing was still scarce but getting quickly better, and the Baby Boom was underway giving much impetus and hope and excitement to the whole population. For the vast majority of people, Australia was a great place to live, and this was a great time to be living here.

Of course, there were some problems. On the international scene, Britain and the Empire were still bound together. So that when England said she was short of US dollars, that meant that we were too. And that meant **we could not buy all of the things from overseas that we wanted**. **Then there were strikes.** Workers wanted a bigger share of the profits that bosses were getting. They also wanted better working conditions than they were afforded. Many of them were prepared to strike for these things. So that strikes, little or big, local or national, well thought-out or capricious, were the bane of everyone's existence. There were other annoyances. Regulations and restrictions and rationing left over from the War still grated. Transport was bad, cars were still hard to get, bank managers were still mean, station masters in country towns were still gods, and the coal scuttle needed emptying. But in all, things had got immeasurably better since the War, and all eyes were now on the happiness that the future would surely bring.

The second matter from the past deals with international matters other than the Chinese Reds. The Berlin Blockade had just finished, and so the Reds on the one hand, and the Allies on the other, **were still keen on being as big a nuisance as they could be to the other side**. And it was the same right round the world. It was a type of foreplay, with each party anxious to see just how far they could go before getting the other really ruffled. Gradually, over the years, both parties toughened up at times, and shook atom bombs at each other, but here we are **now** in 2016 with no nuclear bang yet to brag about. But, back in 1950, there were all sorts of serious conferences going on to avoid such a war, mainly with the intention of showing that no one can push **us** round, whoever **us** might be. And of course, everyone wanted to show that they were the good guys, and that either capitalism or communism was the good cause. We will also return to this theme later in this book.

The third matter from the past comes from the fairy-tale world of Hollywood. Ingrid Bergman, the famous star of *Casablanca*, had gone to the Mediterranean to appear in a picture called *Stromboli*. There she had fallen in love or in lust with Roberto Rossellini, the producer of the film. Their affair had become public. Right now, the whole adventure was coming to a head, and she was seeking a divorce from her husband, and trying to get married to Rossellini, and was expecting his child to be born soon. The Press was busy tut-tutting, and doing what ever it could to inflame the situation. It was all a bit of a mess.

Here we had a lady who was pregnant, and who wanted to just get on with her admittedly-glamorous job of making a movie, and then fade away with Rossellini into the sunset. But there were others with different ideas. There were hundreds of organisations in America, and a few here in Australia, that **threw enormous energy into demonising her.** They held public protests with marches and placards. They wanted to boycott her films, they asked various churches to ex-communicate the couple, they started smear campaigns telling of other horrible things they were said to be guilty of. This was not a run-of the-mill protest. It was a wild scream from a generation of women who were suddenly in fear that the next generation of daughters would follow a similar sinful path, given the influence supposedly exercised by the successful and famous Bergman.

At this point I draw a contrast with what I see in Australia **today**. I know families of six children who have no idea who their respective fathers are. There are families of four children, each clearly with a different father. In some cases, children are born from surrogate dads, or by artificial insemination. At the same time, the nuclear family with a mum and dad and four children is now scarce. It is all a huge change in the last 65 years, and in fact **since** the Baby Boom years. Take one example, again from our American celebrities. Every day we are treated to news items that say that so-and-so is pregnant to someone-or-other. There is no sense of outrage here. It has become like a sport, trying to guess who will be next. It seems **a long way from Bergman**

and Rossellini solemnly admitting to their romance, and facing up to the terrible shame.

I am not wise enough to know if such changes in morality are a good thing or a bad thing. In fact, I don't think that anyone could answer the question. All I can do is put a foot in both camps. Some of the old practices were terrible, like hushing up a "pregnancy out of wedlock." On the other hand, the flamboyant extremes of our current prima donnas are pretty bad too. You had better form your own opinion.

MY RULES IN WRITING

NOTE. In this book, I rely a lot on re-producing Letters from the newspapers. Whenever I do this, I put the text in a different font, and indent it a little, and make the font somewhat smaller. I do not edit the text at all. I do not correct spelling or grammar, and if the text gets at all garbled, I do not correct it. It's straight from the Papers.

SECOND NOTE. The material for this book, when it comes from newspapers, is reported as it was seen at the time. If **hindsight** over the years changes things, then I might record that in **my Comments**. The info reported thus reflects matters as they were seen at the time in 1950.

THIRD NOTE. Let me also apologise in advance to anyone I might offend. In a work such as this, it is certain some people will think I got some things wrong. I am sure that I did, but please remember, all of **this is only my opinion**. And really, my opinion does not matter one little bit in the scheme of things. I hope you will say **"silly old bugger", shrug your shoulders, and read on**.

JANUARY NEWS ITEMS

One of the joys of living in Australia at the moment was that **strikes abounded everywhere**. They could be little ones, only one day, or they could last for a month. They could be planned and notice given a day or two in advance. Or they could be sudden, with workers emptying their water bottles and going home....

At the moment, the wharfies have decided that if everyone else was having their Chrissi holidays, they would do the same. So, for example, 30 ships were idle by January 5th, then 51 by the 7th, and more interstate. **But this is just a small sample...**

When the holidays are over, and people go back to work, **the business of striking in large numbers will become serious again.**

Blackouts were another endless source of annoyance. Coal miners were rather good at striking, and so coal supplies were always low. Any hiccup in delivery to power stations meant that blackouts would immediately occur. On average, **you might expect that** in Sydney, and most other capital cities, **about a quarter of houses and industry would have two hours without power every other day.**

The Communists in China had finished their Revolution and had driven the Nationalist government of Chiang Kai Shek to the island of Formosa. **So that 99 percent of China's population was now governed by the Reds....**

Britain now formally recognised the Reds as the legitimate governors of the land, and was only the fifth nation to do so. The USA was a huge supporter of Chiang Kai Shek, and **refused recognition of Red China until the early 1970's....**

Australia wanted to sell China our goods, especially wheat, but still refused to recognise the nation until the USA did....

The bitterness between the US and China will come to a head in a few months' time in **the Korean War**.

Doctor Pennycuick, of Adelaide University, advised smokers that **18 cigarettes a day would be harmless.** Over 30 would be looking for trouble. Even worse, **smoke 10 in an hour and you are likely to get a fatal dose of nicotine.** There was as yet, **in Australia, little knowledge of the link between cancer and smoking.**

Five years after the end of WWII, about 100 Japanese soldiers will be sent to Manus Island to **face charges relating to war crimes against Australian prisoners.** At the same time, America is trying its own set of villains. There is **no sympathy in Australia for anyone found guilty.**

An English migrant, who arrived here six months ago, was **seen swimming out to sea** at Sydney's famous Bondi Beach. He was far from shore when a surf life-boat caught up with him. He refused to come on board, and **the Captain landed him by his arm and hair**. He was taken to Bondi Police Station and there charged. What was the charge? **Attempting to commit suicide by swimming out to sea.**

DUGAN AND MEARS

The one item that stole the headlines for January and February was the continuing exploits of Darcy Dugan and William Mears. This pair of violent criminals had been in Long Bay Gaol until mid-December, but had escaped in daring circumstances. They had been taken to Central lock-up so that they could answer a charge of armed robbery and, while there, had managed to cut through an iron bar over a door to their cell, which they evacuated in no time at all. They had then walked out of that illustrious police station, and disappeared from sight.

All of this was very galling to the prison authorities and the police. Dugan had been bragging at Long Bay that he would be out by Christmas, and it seemed he had made good on his promise. Then they had cut their way out using a hack-saw, and that opened up ample opportunities for all the old jokes about hack-saws hidden in birthday cakes. It was indeed a great embarrassment to everyone concerned, and the government of the day was not spared either. The police raided all the premises they could think of, and some others that they were given tip-offs about. But in the latter case, they were constantly hampered by the fact that associates of the two escapees were only too happy to call in false information to confuse the issue.

The disappearance of the pair was complete except for one phone call. It was from Mears, who rang a Sydney paper and complained that the police and newspapers were constantly referring to them as "gun-men" whereas, he said, they were not. He went on to say that the police were trying to condition the public to the idea that they **were** gun-men, so that when they were captured, the police could shoot them, and put a bottle of gin by their side, and claim that they committed suicide.

So, the pair remained well hidden until early January. Then, one Saturday night they broke into the home of famous jockey Jack Thompson, and robbed him and his wife at gunpoint, and escaped with a small amount of cash. Thompson was able to run into the street as they left, and discharge a shotgun into the side of their car. But to no avail. They got away.

A week later, the daring duo entered a bank at Ultimo in Sydney. They both jumped up onto the counter, brandishing revolvers, and yelled instructions to everyone to lie down on the floor. The manager reached for the gun in his drawer, and the larger of the two gunmen (Mears) shot him in the chest. He then fired five more shots at random, and hit a customer in the arm.

The second gunman shouted the question "why did you do that?" and they appeared to panic and ran from the bank with no money. They were picked up soon thereafter by a stolen get-away vehicle, driven by a third man, that was later abandoned for another stolen car. The shooting victims were sent to hospital, and recovered.

Police called in every officer possible to help with the man-hunt. They made lightning raids on the homes of relatives and friends of the two men. During the next 24 hours, 1,200 persons were questioned. Over the next few weeks, the search went on, sometimes in the most fanciful manner. For example, on January 30, a Skymaster plane flying from

Melbourne to Sydney radioed ahead to police suspecting that Dugan and Mears were on board.

All available police and suburban patrol cars, in addition to the Eastern and Western wireless patrols and motor-cycle units, covered the aerodrome area. Heavily armed police were stationed at entrances and on the tarmac. The plane was kept circling for twenty minutes until the police were in position. When the plane landed, the passengers were allowed to leave as normal, but only one young man had even the slightest resemblance to Dugan, and all passengers were allowed to leave without any contact with the police. This was just one of the hundreds of false alarms that the police were called on to answer.

On the 4th of February, they struck again. Dugan, armed with a sub-machine gun, and Mears, with a revolver, attempted to rob a pay-roll van as it moved money into dockland premises in Balmain, in Sydney. One guard carrying twelve thousand Pounds ran inside with the money, and Dugan fired at him, wounding him in the leg. The guard got up, and continued to run, taking the money with him. The three other guards fought a gun-battle with the bandits, during which Dugan fired a total of 25 shots. The two men again got into a get-away car, and then into a stolen launch, and made their escape across Sydney Harbour. Police, now armed with sub-machine guns, continued to search for the pair across the city.

The public by now was fully alarmed. Twice within a month these armed robbers had struck, and fired willy-nilly at the public. A *SMH* editorial described them as murderous ruffians, careless of whom they wounded or killed, and called for a state of police emergency; and it opined that such villains were encouraged by the fact that their necks were safe from the rope, and suggested that a complete shake-up of the police force might be necessary. "Every resource of the police department should be mobilised to see that they are brought to book before they have a chance to imperil the lives of peaceful citizens again. Such men deserve no mercy."

Letter-writers were of course vocal. Many offered advice as to how to capture the criminals, and others talked about the roots of crime.

But, suddenly, the jig was up. Their goose was cooked. The party was over, their dash was done justice was served. Their days were numbered, they were lumbered On February 15th the police were happy to report that the two men had been re-captured. Following a tip-off, thirty police had surrounded a house in beachside Collaroy after dark, but it was not until 4.30am on the next day that they invaded the premises. They used a sledge hammer to break down the flimsy back door, and found the two men struggling to get out of a double bed. Dugan tried to hide under it, while Mears simply stood there shivering. They were taken to Central Police Station, from where they had escaped, and charged with a total of 12 offences, including the shootings and armed robberies. A reward of five hundred Pounds was to be paid to the informant.

At their subsequent trial, both men were sentenced to death for shooting with intent to kill. The State Government later commuted this to life imprisonment. Both men were released after 15 years. They each retired into obscurity.

Dugan died in 1992, and Mears in 2002. Dugan's exploits were described by writer Rod Hay in a book entitled "*Catch Me if You Can.*"

H-BOMBS GETTING CLOSER

The Acting Chairman of the US Atomic Energy Commission delivered some cheery news. He now believed that it **would definitely be possible to make hydrogen bombs.** Four scientists working on the project were confident that such a bomb would create enough radioactive dust to kill everyone in the world.

They indicated that harmless chemical elements, like cobalt or carbon, placed in an H-bomb, would turn into radioactive dust when it exploded. It was stated that the use of such bombs in a war would create radioactivity lasting 5,000 years, and that would make life on earth impossible for all that period.

They pointed out that there were still some difficulties with making the bomb effective. For example, the bomb would need to be so big that delivery by plane or rocket would cause problems. They also thought that it could be three more years before the bomb was ready to test. Then, there was the small problem at the moment that to drop a bomb would release devastation over the entire world, and that damage could not yet be restricted to enemy areas.

But everyone was hopeful and confident that solutions to these problems were imminent, and that America would be able to add such bombs to its arsenal in a few years time.

In fact, **it turned out that the first successful design was created in 1951**, and US, Britain and Russia were each able to successfully test a bomb in 1952, and soon thereafter.

And so began a great game of bluff. The goodies told the baddies that whoever dropped the first bomb would get a few back in return. And that was supposed to stop every one from doing this. No one did in fact drop the first bomb, but I am not so sure that this **nuclear** approach was the only reason for this.

Back in February, 1950, quite a few writers were worried about all the success reported above. Here is an impassioned plea that struck a chord with many.

Letter, Joan Lewis. Was the front-page article on the destructive power of the hydrogen bomb just to be swallowed with the bacon and eggs, digested and forgotten as quickly?

Surely, the ordinary people of this world should react violently to such an article. We must feel desperate fear of such an ungodly and monstrous means of destruction, even though we may comfort ourselves that death must come somehow, in some form or other.

Surely, as ordinary humans, no matter what our creed, crimes, or state of culture, we must halt in our tracks, and know, with all that makes us human, that this thing must be stopped.

Such loose talk of world-wide suicide is incredibly fantastic. How could any government of any country feel it worth while to spend countless millions in creating a missile, which, if used, would wipe out all life on this planet, including our own. As a humble housewife, I ask, what could be the point of it all? We might almost laugh at the ghastly and futile absurdity of such an silly idea.

War in itself is a vile thing, retarding human progress in every way. And yet so soon after the last war, we are forced to contemplate the possibility of another war, not to end all war, but to end all life.

What are we to do? Just read about it and carry on? Or can we find a way to stop this crazy career toward universal suicide?

For the sake of all men and women, during all time, who have spent their lives trying to make this a good world to live in, surely, we of this time in history, with our scientific enlightenment and lessons from the past, can do better that destroy all that the centuries have built.

We are only little people, but if we all cry out together perhaps we may be heard.

WHITE AUSTRALIA POLICY

Australia was firmly attached to this policy in 1950. But in 1949, it had been shocked and revolted by the extreme manner in which it had been enforced. Arthur Calwell, the then-Minister for Immigration, had refused to make exceptions to our Immigration laws in respect of Asians who had entered the country during the War. The result was that the most inhumane deportation of hundreds of persons was done without regard for any mitigating factor.

Now, under the new Menzies Government, the new Minister for External Affairs, Percy Spender, was being approached to make such an exception in the case of a resident of Ceylon. This person, a Mr Trench, was a British subject of Burgher descent, and satisfied the requirement that he be of at least 75 per cent European extraction. But, along with other Burghers, he was of darker appearance than normal Europeans, and so he did not satisfy the requirement that he be "preponderantly of European appearance." His brother was of a lighter colour, and he had been accepted by Mr

Calwell two years earlier, but our Mr Trench was rejected
– **purely on his colour, and not at all on race.**

At the end of January, Mr Spender was confronted with
this situation, and he elected to consider it. By March, he
had made the determination that Mr Trench could enter
Australia as a migrant. This of course was an important
decision, because it signalled **the beginning of a new,
more liberal, interpretation of our hitherto inflexible
policies on immigration.**

POLIO EPIDEMIC WAS STARTING

The nation had been under threat for three years from the
rising incidence of polio, a disease that resulted in the death
or crippling of children. Every parent, as soon as a child
developed certain symptoms, had an immediate fear that it
might be polio. In 1950, the plague still had over a decade
to run, and it was not until the development of the Salk
and Sabin vaccines in the next decade that the disease was
conquered.

NEWS AND VIEWS

As January drew to a close, holiday-makers gradually
returned to work and to the cities, forgot all their New-
Year's resolutions, and faced up to the year ahead. Over the
next few pages, I include a small glimpse of the world that
they came back to. This is a pattern I will generally stick to
in this book. That is, I will **close** most Chapters with **a few
pages of scattered news-items and Letters,** some of them
trivial, some quite weighty, and expect and hope that they
give you various glimpses of times gone by.

Beer by the Bottle. Letters, FAIRNESS. My husband is a permanent invalid of the First World War and in the last four years it has been impossible to buy an **odd bottle of beer** for him to offer his visitors. He does not drink himself.

It is high time the housewife could purchase a single bottle occasionally from her grocer, whoever he may be. The few licensed grocers, when approached, can supply every brand of wine, but the bottle of beer is an unknown quantity.

Care of our stamps. Letters, J Leslie. Our postage stamps could be silent but very effectively publicity agents for Australia, and would be if they were allowed to function properly.

This is particularly true of those which bear pictures of our fauna. Here is something peculiarly Australian and, in the main, very well depicted. But often the stamps are so brutally treated in canceling that the device is almost obliterated by blobs of carbon black suggestive of the shearing shed tarpot. To leave only a head or a tail showing is poor treatment to accord our beloved kookaburra or famed lyre-bird. And it is scant honour to the engraver's good work.

By this defacement, the cancellation, as a date mark, is rendered illegible, and so is useless from this point of view. A light line would cancel the stamp just as well, and at the same time spare the little messenger to render its tacit but valuable service.

Wastage of police time? Letters, William Hulme. Last week, I witnessed three Crown sergeants, plus motor car and driver, inspecting hotels for chipped glasses etc. Then we have hundreds of police hunting down SP bookies, inoffensive Chinese refugees, and two-up players having their little gamble in places affecting nobody. We also see fleets of motor cars and trucks, with many police in each, hunting round hotels and arresting citizens – mostly those who are not drunk. If these hundreds of police were assigned to tracking down real criminals, there would be less crime and more respect for the police force.

Dollar Pool, News Item. Miss Betty Sterling, winner of the Manly Mardi Gras competition, will not be able to leave Sydney today for Fiji and America, if the Commonwealth persists in its hard line. She has no shortage of money to pay for the trip, because this was raised by the competition. The problem is that she cannot get Commonwealth Bank permission **to spend the US dollars** that the trip requires.

Australia is linked to Britain by the dollar pool, and we have regulations that limit spending of our currency in dollar areas, because this results in a dollar drain. The Treasurer, Arthur Fadden, indicated today that permission would not be granted to spend dollars for purposes of pleasure, which was how this trip was classified.

Miss Sterling said that she felt sure that the trip would only be postponed for a few days. She added, diplomatically, that "I don't want to go if it means taking dollars from Australia." Late tonight it was reported that a resident of Hawaii had responded to her plight, and made a pledge to provide the necessary dollars.

Hopes for cream, News item. There have been strong rumours from reliable sources that Federal Cabinet is expected to soon lift the ban on the sale of cream. Since early in the War, cream has been available to consumers only if they held a doctor's certificate verifying that their health demanded it. It has taken ten years and a change of government for authorities to realise that the ban was not achieving its purpose.

FEBRUARY NEWS ITEMS

The Federal Government had in mind that **our population was pitifully small** if we were to protect ourselves against invaders. There were supposed to be **half a dozen nations to our north salivating at the prospect of getting our natural resources**. We had to "**populate or perish**", was the cry....

So the Government decided to give more money to encourage the formation of larger families. It now said that **child endowment would be paid to the first child in the family.** Previously it had been paid only to the second and subsequent child. **This was a sizeable bounty**, and families were pleased to get it. **It is dubious if it in any way increased our population.** After all, we were in the middle of the Baby Boom. **Most patriots were already doing their bit.**

The Minister for Trade and Customs has ordered an enquiry into **the number of cigarette lighters being imported** into this nation. He had observed that these **lighters pay no import tax, while matches pay sales tax**. He thinks there are a million lighters in Australia, and noted that the biggest match-maker made a loss last financial year. He is likely to **prop up the match-makers by imposing customs duties on lighters....**

This was a fairly typical attitude at the time. That is, **protect our local industries in dying trades** rather than encourage the growth of local industries that could stand open competition.

The *SMH* will issue a free 16-page supplement next week. It will contain unusual and **up-to-date-designs for jumpers and cardigans**, Fair-Isle patterned, plain patterned and striped. **Interest in knitting was high**, and sales of knitting needles and wool were booming. **Good news from America.** A hydrogen-bomb will be ready for testing in 1952. **More good news.** It will be tested **in the Pacific**, presumably so that we can get a good look at it. Maybe we can get some good fall-out from it. That is something **we should all look forward to. Life can be beautiful....**

Albert Einstein saw it differently. He abhorred the arms race and talked about **the annihilation of all human life**. He fumed about the development of H-bombs by the USA and Russia "with feverish pace", and noted that every step seems to lead to the ultimate destruction of life on the planet....

Einstein's dire warnings were taken more seriously than similar statements from Presidents and world leaders. They were playing politics. Einstein was seen as a **scientist who knew what he was talking about.** In those days, scientists were trusted as being objective. After Einstein spoke, **many ordinary people slept less soundly** than before, for quite a few years.

Fresh cream still may not be sold in Australia. All the cream is supposed to be used for **producing butter for Britain.** Reports from Britain indicate that there is now plenty of butter there, so that our own producers are making **fresh pleas to have the ban lifted.**

PETROL RATIONING

On February 8th, Prime Minister Menzies announced that **petrol rationing** in Australia would be abandoned immediately. In a broadcast to the nation, he said that the Government had been able to procure supplies of petrol from regions in the Sterling currency area, and that getting the extra supplies would not run down our dollar balances.

He said that where supplies were needed from dollar sources, our reserves of dollars were in fact adequate to cope. We do not need to worry about the British dollar pool. **We can mange our own resources and let Britain manage theirs.**

This was a major policy change for the new Government. On the one hand, it repudiated the **Chifley** claim that non-dollar sources could not be found. But it also went against the wishes of Britain which was anxious that we should regard the dollar pool as being a single pool that the entire Empire was party to. **The idea of individual countries like Australia running their own dollar accounts was quite unpleasant to it.**

But as Menzies put it explicitly, "I am aware that the British Government would have liked us to reach a different conclusion from the one I have announced tonight. But this move fully recognises our right to determine for ourselves the reason for which we choose to spend our dollars." He went on to say that the annual cost of administering the scheme had been 600,000 Pounds, which was the equivalent of nine million gallons of petrol.

Comment. Over the next few decades, Australia's allegiance to Britain slowly diminished, until today we are very independent from her, and indeed many are questioning even the link to the monarchy. Commentators over the years have looked at just **when** Australia started to move away from Britain. I think that **this** decision of Menzies was the first definite sign that such a move was afoot. Of course, Menzies turned out to be a lover of all things British, and the most vigorous supporter of the monarchy. Nevertheless, I consider that it was this decision to buck British dictates over petrol imports that set a precedent that at first gradually, and then rapidly, grew into moves from the entire Empire for financial self-determination.

MRS O'KEEFE: WHITE AUSTRALIA

One of the major controversies of the previous year had been over an Indonesian woman, Mrs O'Keefe. She and her first husband had been active during the War **in fighting the Japanese in their occupation of Indonesia**. The Japanese had learned of their activities, and had sent a patrol to capture her. **The Australian navy realised this, and evacuated her, and her seven children, to Australia.** This was in 1942. Her husband had been subsequently killed fighting the Japanese, and she had re-married an Australian towards the end of the War.

In 1949, the Immigration Department, led by Arthur Calwell, was intent on maintaining the purity of Australian blood, and was throwing out any Asians who had migrated here during the War. They claimed that O'Keefe fitted into that category. The counter-claim was that she had come in as a refugee, and was thus not subject to laws regarding migrants. The High Court of Australia agreed with her, and said she could stay.

At this point, Calwell could have simply let O'Keefe off the hook, and granted her an exemption on humanitarian grounds. But, on the contrary, he instead passed the Wartime Refugees Act that made it possible to deport **all** persons who had entered during the War. **This was obviously aimed at removing O'Keefe and others.** But before he could enforce the new Act, elections had come and he had been tossed out as the Minister.

Now, in February 1950, the new Minister for Immigration, in a widely popular move, granted the O'Keefes the exemption they so badly wanted, and allowed them to remain in the country. This put an end to an episode which for long had tainted our relationships with all the other countries in Asia. Fortunately, while it did not remove the White Australia Policy (WAP), it placed its interpretation on a more humane basis, and made it not quite the same source of Asian resentment as it had been under the previous administration.

Not everyone agreed with this decision.

Letters, W Wallis. It is reported that the Rev Alan Walker said that, in its decision on the O'Keefe case, the Government had expressed the will of the people.

I think that what Mr Walker meant to say was that the vast majority of Australians with whom **he** associates approve this decision. But I can assure him that the vast majority of Australians with whom **I** come into contact are utterly disgusted with this decision. **The woman should go.**

I am not too sure that some of them, if they had to vote today, may not vote differently to what they did on December 10th last.

In any case, there was still plenty to complain about in our WAP.

Letters Brian Dooley. The announcement of the Minister for the Army that **only white residents** will be enlisted in the **Papua-New Guinea Militia** is regrettable, unless a separate native Militia is to be formed also. Surely the native people should be given the opportunity of training **to defend their own country**. The war record of the Papuan Infantry Battalion was splendid.

The loyalty and courage of the natives have been shown, too, in the Royal Papuan Constabulary. Native ex-Servicemen have been a tower of strength among Christians in the Anglican missionary area. It was the Papuan Christians who were "the fuzzy-wuzzy angels."

Now any discrimination against the native people must hamper the efforts of the missionaries and encourage the Communists to spread their own propaganda. The Papuans have been faithful friends and gallant allies. Without them, we cannot defend New Guinea. Let us show them that we still trust them.

TALKING OF FOREIGNERS

There were other forces at work with **European foreigners**. **Their accents** came up for discussion in a letter to the *Herald*, and that opened a can of worms. The situation then was very different from what it is today. Migrants from Europe were pouring into the nation, but these persons were definitely of working class origin, and had no pretension to wealth. On the other hand, all the writers of the letters below were from Sydney's very affluent Eastern suburbs, and were quite remote from the New Australians being housed in the old army barracks round the nation.

Remember too that during the War, Germans and Italians across Australia were generally interned, and that conversation **in their languages** had been taboo for the war-years, and that all was not yet forgiven. Even the French had sometimes been seen as luke-warm in their support of the Allies, so that the French language too was a bit suspect in some minds. So the net result was that **vocal** people with "heavy" foreign accents were quite scarce, and, it appears, were sometimes given a hard time by the locals.

Letters, Mrs A Rottberg. It is high time that people stopped criticising the way foreigners speak English. Almost every day I read in your paper "he spoke with a heavy foreign accent", etc.

As it is a known fact that 99.9 per cent of the Australians can't even say "yes" in another language, I find this criticism very impertinent.

And what of it, if foreigners speak in their own native tongue, even in public? British people especially, when living abroad, hardly ever learn the language of their adopted country, give their children English Christian names, and hardly ever get naturalised. Why should they have these privileges and not the foreigners also, who live here? **Low class** landladies, greengrocers, tram conductors, and suburban housewives are most ferocious in their criticism. It is time they stopped.

Letters, G Lefevbre. Mrs Rottberg takes exception to "low class" people criticising foreign accents. British people freely admit that they are hopeless linguists, and your correspondent would do well to emulate their recognised ability to laugh cheerfully at themselves in this matter. I suspect that Mrs Rottberg's angry bridlings are the direct result of a painful lack of any sense of humour.

I prescribe a course of the British magazine "Punch", taken at regular intervals. Alternatively, she should immediately take up residence, either in the country of her origin, where presumably she will be linguistically safe, or in some other unfunny land whose Kommissar for Kulture bans all criticism as being unprogressive.

As for her absurd statement that 99.9 percent of Australians are unable to say "yes" in any other language, Mrs Rottberg is obviously misinformed. Because of their geographical position, there is no reason why they should, but the fact remains that many Australians are eagerly learning foreign languages, even though they know their accents often leave much to be desired.

With deliciously unconscious humour, your correspondent mentions greengrocers, an enormous percentage of whom are far more proficient in saying "yes" in Italian , Greek, or Chinese than in English.

Letters, Mrs A Rottberg. Myself and my family, and many friends among them including quite a few French, have been repeatedly ridiculed and abused on account of our accents. And these abuses came always from **the lower classes of the population**, who are badly educated and whose criticism I resent very much.

I came to Australia in 1933 from Bern in Switzerland, and during these 16 years I didn't find one Australian who could converse in one of my three mother tongues, namely German, French or Italian.

The fact remains that the Britisher living abroad never bothers to speak some other language but exclusively English. Whether they like being criticised by other people is very doubtful. What I claim is only the same privilege for the foreigners living here.

Letters, A FORMER AUSTRIAN. As a former Austrian and now British subject, I agree that in many instances

I too have noticed the criticism of "foreign accents" by Australians through the Press and otherwise. But, if the criticism is done by ignorant people, then I in turn ignore it. If however it is a matter of interest on the Australian's part, which it mostly is, then I don't object to their mentioning it.

A certain type of person can be found in almost every country who will always criticise others. If it gives them satisfaction, then I wish them good luck. But personally I find that mixing with Australians is the best remedy to break down any prejudice that they may have against "foreign" people and accents. Certainly the great distance which separates Australia from the European countries must have some bearing on this subject.

To those "non-Australians" who feel the criticism so strongly I can only say ignore the rude and impertinent. One cannot re-educate them, but luckily they do not constitute the whole population of Australia.

Letters, INTERESTED AUSTRALIAN. As the Australian wife of a naturalised "foreigner" who has been in Australia for 35 years, I heartily concur with Mrs Rottberg. One fact that seems to be completely overlooked by so many people is that Englishmen and Australians are themselves "foreigners" when abroad. The average Australian, unfortunately, has little chance of travel owing to the distance which separates us from both USA and Europe restricting such costly pleasure. We are therefore rather narrow in outlook and even intolerant in some ways.

Why not mix with these people and try to help them a little. We could learn much from them – another language, delicious cooking, and charming embroideries, to mention just a few items. This would be of benefit to us, and would be much kinder than ridiculing them as some are prone to do. Complete understanding might be achieved if we reversed the position and imagined ourselves in a similar position.

Letters, Stanley Greenland. It is perhaps the arrogant demeanour of some of our New Australians which irks the old hands, rather than the quaintness of their tongues.   Mrs Rottberg must forgive me if I find her guilty of intolerance and arrogance. I, too, am a foreigner, an elderly Englishman, who by reason of the exigencies of war found sanctuary in this great sunny land to my great content, despite the fact that my particular accent calls forth many a jibe and jape from my Australian contemporaries – jibes and japes which my common sense tells me carry no barbed or poisoned shafts.

I live in a part of Sydney which is lively with the languages of Europe other than English. I have often walked the streets and can understand all sorts of European languages. I have, on occasions, been shocked by the snatches of conversations I have heard. Many European "foreigners" are grateful to be here, but others seem to have forgotten the horrors and miseries that were there in their homelands.

These latter people must not be surprised if the nimble-witted Australians are quick to take notice. Mrs Rottberg must have been hibernating if, indeed, she is serious that during 16 years she failed to find one Australian who could converse in either German, French or Italian.

Remark. There is no doubt that Australians at this time were inclined to be somewhat xenophobic, much more than they are now. **In 2016,** in our cities in particular, but also on labour sites and elsewhere, there is such as mixture of nationalities that the person who resents them is truly a relic. But in 1950, the general attitude was basically that European foreigners were different, perhaps strange, perhaps not to be fully trusted. Still it is hard to see any direct antagonism towards them. And I think that our Mrs Rottberg, from Vaucluse, was out of step with most foreigners living here as well, and that most of them could cope with our querulousness better than she managed to do.

CHARLIE CHAPLIN SEEKS REFUGE

The Hollywood funny-man needed ongoing help around 1950. During the 1940's, his **left-wing stance was seen by many as being favourable to Communism.** By 1947, when he produced the movie, *Monsieur Verdoux*, many US cities black-listed it because of his supposed Red-ness. By 1952, when he briefly visited his homeland England, **Edgar Hoover (FBI) cancelled his return visa**. Chaplin sought comfort in eastern Europe, and said he would never return to the US. He did, once, to receive an Honorary Oscar.

NEWS AND VIEWS

Letters, Michael Sawtell. These heavy rains outback are not altogether unexpected by old and experienced bushmen. It is the firm conviction of many who have lived in Central Australia for a number of years that once Lake Eyre is full, there will follow a cycle of good years for the region.

Last year, all the creeks and rivers in the Lake Eyre basin flooded and filled the Lake. I crossed the Cooper at Coppramanna and saw the river three miles wide, gently flowing into Lake Eyre. More water ran into Lake Eyre, in the so-called "Dead Heart" of Australia, than is in Sydney Harbour.

The experience of a full Lake Eyre influencing the rainfall gave rise to the suggestion of cutting a channel at Port Augusta and allowing the sea to flood much of the Centre, which is about 39 feet below sea-level. Many years ago this would have been a formidable task, but now with modern earth-moving equipment, it would be quite easy.

Some scientists sneer at this proposal, but after 50 years experience of the vast inland, I am sure that the proposal is sound.

Letters, NATURALIST. Why, in the name of all that is rational and decent, should Taronga Park have ten rhinoceroses?

Is it that the controllers relish boasting that they have "more than any other zoo in the world"? Or is it that they expect the death-roll among the luckless animals to be high? Either or both of these considerations would seem to prevail strongly at Taronga Zoo nowadays, for the place is badly overcrowded with various kinds of mammals and birds.

Obviously, the buying of at least eight more rhinos than the zoo needs, to say nothing of the cost involved in feeding all of these unfortunates, represents an outlay that could easily have been devoted to some much more useful purpose.

Letters, G De Lissa. The five Pound booking fee being charged by the rich and mighty GPS school called *Shore* is a good idea. If all GPS schools introduced this, then it might prevent certain people **registering their children at all GPS schools at birth,** as is now the case, and then simply taking the favoured one later. They then cancel the other ones. Such a charge might stop them and end up with a fairer system.

You are a Brit again. The Minister for Immigration, Mr Harold Holt, announced to-day that from July 1st, Australian passports will again bear the inscription "British

Passport." The words were dropped last year by the Chifley government, but will now appear again under Menzies.

Mr Holt stated that, by removing the words "British" from the passports, travellers were sometimes denied the benefits of British citizenship because not all people who inspected passports were aware of the links between Australia and Great Britain

Further, he went on to say, Australians were proud to be part of the British Empire, and wanted to be seen as such.

Happy days for hens. News Item. Reports from various poultry studies confirm that **hens kept in cages lay more eggs** and put on more weight than hens who run free.
This could revolutionise the industry with lower costs and higher revenue. Surely the world will be a better place.

Do you remember black school shoes? They were made of incredibly stiff leather, and they were always bought a size too small, so that they would stretch. When they got holes in them, did you either put kromide on them, or take them to the cobbler to get them half-soled? Did you get hand-me-downs from an older sibling? Did you get through primary school without wearing shoes? In sixth class, did you get a pair of white Dunlop sand shoes that were so light and care-free that you walked on air for weeks?

Well, maybe yes; or maybe no. In any case, **guess who did**.

The famous pianist **Hephzibah** Menuhin was highly critical of TV in America. She said that children there sit watching blood-curdling TV, and chewing gum. They are lazy, lethargic, and completely lacking in initiative. She commended Australia for not yet having TV in their homes.

On Monday night, at the Sydney Stadium, our Empire Middleweight Champion Dave Sands beat British challenger Olson on points. **Here is another reminder of a world that has changed.** In 1950, for sporting fans round the nation, the **Monday night fights were not to be missed. Radios broadcast every blow**, bets were placed at thousands of **SP bookies,** and a few thousand were lucky enough to get into the stadium. **A different world.**

A Melbourne woman is making **an expensive appeal to the Privy Council in England**. After she left a hospital with a baby in 1945, she became convinced that she had the wrong baby. She took the matter to the Supreme Court in Victoria and it said that **she was right in her suspicion**. Another woman objected to this and won a High Court appeal **against the decision.** Now the matter will go before the Privy Council. **Note that the ultimate court in Australia was still the Privy Council in England.**

American anthropologist **Margaret Mead** announced today that she would like to go and live with a tribe of Australian aborigines for a time, to do research. It was not immediately known if the aborigines also wanted her.

Have you had a **pink** fit recently? Are you feeling in the **pink**? Are you still tickled **pink** by something? **Question:** where did all this **pink**ness come from? Where did it go?

MARCH NEWS ITEMS

A New Jersey firm has placed on sale a toy kit for **children** that allows them to **monitor radio-activity** near the home. It included a **Geiger counter** and some metal with a small radiation for playing with. It also has instructions on **what to do if an atom-bomb is dropped** in their back yard, as well as a list of provisions they need to **stock their air-raid cellar for a month.**

An atomic physicist Dr Klaus Fuchs was sentenced to **14 years in prison in Britain for passing research information to the Russians** over a period of seven years. This was the beginning of **spy trials and chases that kept security forces occupied for the next decade.** Countless novels were written, hundreds of persons gaoled, and millions of rooms were bugged. You might remember the **famous Burgess and Maclean and their Cambridge friends.**

Five lifesavers from Sydney's Bondi beach were to compete in a surf-boat carnival in **Coolangatta, 700 miles away**. To get their boat there, **they took the obvious course and rowed it up the coast**....

On a 25-mile stage from Terrigal to Newcastle, they were accompanied by **a pack of 15 large sharks which kept circling the boat. The largest of these was 20 feet long**, and the others were smaller, "only 15 feet." At one stage the boat looked like swamping, but "we rowed it out."

The **world's worst airline tragedy - to date** - occurred near Britain's Cardiff. **Eighty people** were killed. Sad to say, this number would **scarcely rate a mention today in some parts of the world.**

The front page of the *SMH* carried a snippet that said that **King George VI had experienced a small headache** while inspecting the Irish Guards. He has taken medical advice, and the Palace was happy to report that **he suffered from a "spring chill"**, with no sign of crippling influenza....

The comings and goings of Royalty were big news in Australia. Our loyalty to the Crown was whole-hearted, and our allegiance to the Empire was still part and parcel of our **British** heritage....

Though that **was about to diminish somewhat** as we encouraged the so-called *Poles and Balts* to migrate. But at this instant, we were **still True Blue and the best parts of the world were still coloured pink**....

Is this the same **pink** that I mentioned earlier?

Does anyone remember when **kids used to swamp the grounds at sporting fixtures**? Sometimes to kick a ball round. Sometimes to inspect the pitch. That has been replaced by barbed wire and security staff. **Progress ain't all good.**

One of our most popular imports at the time was Chief Little Wolf, a US wrestler. He came here often at this time, and was very popular with the crowds, with **his headband of giant feathers, and his royal fatness**. He was famous for his **Step-Over-Toe-Hold**, but especially for the **Indian-Death-Lock**, his own wrestling creation.

DUGAN AND MEARS IN COURT

The infamous couple were brought before the court for **a committal hearing,** which simply tested whether there was sufficient evidence to bring them to trial by jury. Police had ultimately decided that 18 charges could be brought against them for their crime spree, but in this initial hearing, only three would be presented. These related to the robbery of jockey Jack Thompson and his wife.

Much of the early evidence told of the actual capture of the pair. Mears, at that time, had made a written confession admitting involvement in the Thompson robbery and other crimes, and **now** claimed that force had been used on him to extract that confession. The police, led by **Detective Ray Kelly**, who throughout his career was never accused of spoiling prisoners, denied this. Mears talked about being held down on the floor, and police putting their knee in his stomach so that he became unconscious. He also talked about being struck with a rubber hose that left no visible damage. He asked Kelly, during cross-questioning, "how did I write the statement freely when I had handcuffs on? I was kicked while I still had handcuffs on – kicked like a dog. A man can stand so much, but I had a gun in the back of my neck, and guns down my throat."

Kelly, and other officers, denied any measure of coercion, and described the questioning of Mears as a quite civilised affair, with Mears starting the interview by saying that he had been just then preparing to give himself up. The Prison Doctor said that there had been only trivial evidence of injury to Mears, and that he had not considered it serious enough to call in another doctor.

Dugan had been questioned separately. He had become anxious and agitated when he found the Mears had signed a statement, and was quoted by several police officers as instructing Mears to retract it. One officer stated he had heard Dugan say "you fool. If you hadn't made those written statements, as we'd agreed, we'd be all right. Now we have to get over your writing the statements. When you get to court, you will have to say you were bashed and kicked into making those statements. You want to make a real squeal to the magistrate about it. That is our only real chance at all."

Dugan was right there. In the case of the Thompson robbery, evidence was based on the say-so of the two victims, who saw the robbers in a darkened room, and only one had his face showing. Without the confession, there could have been room for doubt. But, try as he might, Mears was up against the fact that it was his word against that of about 20 police officers, and it turned out that the magistrate believed the officers. They were both committed for trial, at a date to be determined.

As an aside: When the two robbers started to search the Thompson's bedroom, one of the men asked Mrs Thompson where she kept her jewellery. She replied that it was on the dressing table. She asked him not to take her wedding ring. He replied "All right, Mrs Thompson. I won't." And he didn't. What a gentleman.

THREE SOCIAL IRRITANTS

No matter what progress is made, there always seem to be some irritating aspects of life that persist, despite all logic.

Here I have given a sample of **three** that were prominent at the time.

First irritant. Letters, Bernie Gilmore. I recently spent three weeks on the road selling, and I stayed in twelve country pubs just West of the ranges. I can say that of the twelve, twelve were hardly fit to live in. First let me say that half the pubs I went to offered no accommodation, except to a handful of drunks.

But of the ones I got into, there were often no hot showers, no evening meals, and no reading room or guests parlour. The rooms were small, grubby, poorly lit so you could not read, and the stink of previous travellers was awful. I had to walk down the corridor to get to a lavatory, which always stank and was generally filthy. The rooms were noisy, especially from about nine o'clock to midnight as the illegal drinkers came in for some black beer. The publicans had mainly been culled from herds of swine.

I can't live like this. Can you imagine taking your family to one of these places? I have given up my job.

Second   irritant.   Letters,   Reginald   Stewart. Doubtless most of your readers will recall the heat and uncomfortable humidity of Sydney last Saturday week. And doubtless, most of your readers were attired in clothing more befitting an Arctic explorer than intelligent natives of a sub-tropical continent.

Having no wish myself to appear as a fugitive from Byrd's Expedition on such a delightfully warm day, I walked about the metropolis immaculately dressed in a linen jacket, shirt and shorts, and stockings.

At mid-day, feeling somewhat in need of an alcoholic stimulant, I instinctively made my way to the lounge of one of Sydney's less uncivilised hotels, accompanied by my wife. But, no sooner had we made ourselves comfortable on a settee, than the head waiter approached, and in all seriousness, asked me to leave simply because I was not wearing a tie.

Greatly astonished, I pointed out that I had recently worn the same clothes in the best hotels in Africa and Singapore, but to no avail. I had to leave.

And, as we were leaving, he informed my wife, who was virtually naked, that she could remain if she so desired.

I have since thought about my humiliating ejection, but I cannot for the life of me see how the wearing of smart commonsense clothing should disqualify one from imbibing among a lot of tie-bound cowboys in the lounge of a second-rate hotel. So long as such ridiculous rules obtain here, Australia will continue to be laughed at from abroad.

Third irritant. War widows. News Item. The annual meeting of the Australian Legion of Ex-servicemen highlighted the poor treatment that war widows received. Mr F Pepper told the meeting of various problems.

The way investigators operate is shocking, War widows are not allowed to live a life of their own. They are under constant scrutiny to decide if they are "living immorally", and anonymous letters are being sent to the Repatriation Department asking them to act on flimsy evidence. **If they are found guilty of living immorally, then their pension is cut off.**

The only chance a widow has of re-marrying is to ask a man into her home. Although this is dangerous, she is too frightened to be seen outside with him.

The investigators, working in pairs, have been known to knock on a widow's door at mid-night. They pull out drawers searching for evidence of immorality. Her children are awakened, and her neighbours immediately brand her.

ACCREDITATION OF MIGRANTS

With the advent of large numbers of migrants to Australia, we had to face up to a new problem. That is, granted that numbers of these New Australians had good professional qualifications, how were we to decide who should be admitted to practice in Australia, and what extra qualifications they would need before registration.

There was general recognition that, for University-trained foreigners, they should attend some teaching at our local Universities, and pass some exams. But all sorts of considerations then came into play. For example, most professional groups are loath to admit too many new members because it would weaken their own positions. Or there was concern that some institutions, which granted some **overseas** degrees, were not up to Australian standards. There were many different reasons.

Take the case of 15 New Australians who had been practising overseas. Each of them had been forced to do the six years of training to get their Australian degree. But they were not naturalised, so they were not automatically qualified here.

The problem was our rules said that only eight of them were allowed to practice in NSW. So the other seven if fact went to New Guinea. Of course, all was not lost for them. There were several ways that they could work their way back into NSW over a few years. But it does highlight the problems that all professions faced at that time. And, I should add, it is a problem that still vexes all the professions right to this very day.

THE H-BOMB: COMING SOON?

There was a large response to **Mrs Lewis' thoughtful Letter**. It is a reflection of the times that **nearly all of those published contained a religious theme**. This should not be too surprising, because the Christian religion played a much more important role in society then than it appears to now. For example, and I am now jumping ahead a few years, when TV arrived here, every channel on every night closed the day with at least five minutes of sermon and prayers. Clergymen and others were noting with great sorrow that church attendances were down, but not with any consciousness that this situation was here to stay, and that, in fact, it would get much worse.

So, the three typical Letters below each contain a religious reference. The first of these is entertainingly jaundiced, but the other two show clearly how those writers were living with a strong active-Christian perspective.

Letters, Gaione Carrington. A number of scientists have asserted that if the world was raided with H-bombs, all life and vegetation would disappear.

What would that matter? All human beings now alive will be dead within 150 years at the most. If all vanished now, there would be no one to miss them.

It is doubtful if human beings have done anything to help the Creator.

Letters, A Robson. When you published the poignant letter of Mrs Lewis, you did a great service to all those who feel deeply the things she said, but could not find words to adequately express them.

The answer to her cry, surely, is not a simple one. Our greed, our stupidity, and lack of imagination, our apathy, these are the factors upon which the present sorry state of the world is largely consequent. It is enough to fill us with despair.

Yet despair need not be the last word. It lies within our power, if we so desire, to make the familiar world we inhabit more worthy of habitation for those who aspire to be rational and are capable of love. Our limitation is due not to ignorance, but to the feebleness of our desire for good.

Some scientists believe that the very science which made the hydrogen bomb possible contains within it a moral ethic which must regard the good of man as a whole as the ultimate goal. Dr C Waddington of Christ's College, Cambridge, has good reason for hope in science itself. But science is moving at too great a speed for us to depend on this. **Surely we must call in the aid of religion.** A new birth of religion is needed if we are to use science for good ends rather than destruction.

Letters, Laura Bolton. I warmly support Mr Robson on the H-bomb. He voices a great truth when he says that science minus religion is scarcely to be trusted.

Our one hope lies in a return to God, for the soulless use of His creative dynamics for purposes of unimaginable and unpredictable mass slaughter, destruction, and pillage can only end one way, as Professor Einstein has told us.

Let us return to God and His wise laws before it is too late, for in those very controls, which some among us find so irksome, lies the whole epitome of successful and lasting nationhood.

NEWS AND VIEWS

If you want to know the time. The Post-Master General runs the nation's post offices, and also the telephone services. It has introduced a new method for customers to find the time.

You can dial up a number, and hear a recorded voice tell you what time it is at your location. Even if you are in Western Australia, the time will be correct.

This is done by wonderful new voice recording devices. A young woman records all possible times, and then they are played back at just the right pace to give you a constant and correct time. This meant that batteries of young women, formerly answering calls, were displaced.

It was an example of wonderful new labour-saving devices, taking over jobs. A new word was just entering our vocabulary. It was "**automation**".

The PMG got away with it this time, but from here on, every **new step towards automation was strongly resisted by the Trade Unions**.

Roberto Rossellini in the news. Ingrid Bergman's lover kept popping up. Here he is in two different contexts.

Firstly, on March 13th, he won a prestigious award, called the Rome Cinema Prize, worth about seven thousand Pounds, for his direction of the film "*Stromboli*", which stars Ingrid Bergman.

But then, he had a more dubious honour. Remember that earlier I mentioned that some worried groups in the US were demonising Bergman and Rossellini. Here is a good example, coming from a US Senator. Rossellini and Bergman had applied for custody of Bergman's daughter from her previous marriage.

Washington, news item. The film director Rossellini was last night vilified by US Senator Edwin C Johnson **on the floor of the Senate.**

He alleged that Rossellini was a drug addict, who associated with an international gang of dope smugglers. The gang, he said, smuggled dope into Hollywood from Red Communist sources in China.

He went on to say "this Nazi collaborator, this black market operator, this associate of drug-smugglers, this bed-room prowler inspired by cocaine, is now asking a Californian court to tear a sweet little American schoolgirl from her devoted father, and turn her over to him to rear."

For the record, Bergman was granted custody of the child only in school holidays. Rossellini was never under any serious suspicion for the matters raised by the Senator.

News Item, Peter Dawson, March 23. Peter Dawson, famous in Australia for his rich baritone voice, had inspired the nation with his singing of *"On the Road to Mandalay"* **during WWII.**

Thus he was well regarded here. But he had an enemy. The Australian Taxation Department. It was dogged in its determination that he should cough up his back taxes, and its long arm harassed`him wherever his singing engagements took him.

He said today from London that **he was broke**. "Everywhere I go, I come back to the Taxation Department that says I owe them money. I cannot estimate how much I earn when I am in a country, and I can't pay tax before I leave because they do not know the amount.

"When I land back, they present me with a bill, and I am supposed to know how much it is and I don't have the money with me for instant payment.

"I hate travel at my age, but I have to do it to put me financially square. Air travel, hotels and moving put a great financial strain on me."

Dawson recorded 2,500 songs that sold 13 million copies. He published his autobiography, entitled "50 Years of Song", in 1951. He died in 1961 at Dee Why in Sydney.

Eugene Goossens in the Park. The world-renowned orchestra conductor appeared before a crowd of 21,000 in an **open air concert** in Sydney. Such Concerts became very popular at the time, as did **the Proms in the evenings**.

For Rugby League lovers. The English Rugby League Team toured Australia in 1950. **On a personal note,** let me say that I was 16 years of age in 1950, and, at the time was well disposed towards England, and all Englishmen. Except these eighteen players who were my sworn enemies.

News Item, London, April 22. Tonight, the King and Queen visited Shakespeare's famous Stratford-upon-Avon. It was the first visit by a reigning monarch in 386 years. After watching *"Henry VIII"*, the Queen requested that **the champagne** that had been readied for their reception **be replaced by tea**. The glasses and magnums were quickly removed, and the entire gathering of 200 people were served a cup of tea.

APRIL NEWS ITEMS

The team of **five lifesavers** who set out to row from **North Bondi to Surfers Paradise arrived there today to a tumultuous reception**. The trip had covered a distance of **570 miles**, and had taken about four weeks. They had some wind assistance for the journey, using a small jib at times....

On arrival, three were suffering from boils, and one went to hospital for a leg injury. **All were vastly tired, and agreed "never again"**.

Does anyone else remember Selfridges? This was **a chain of retail stores**, and their competition was Coles. Then **Selfridges was taken over by Coles**, leaving that chain to become the giant that it is today. It was **years later that Woolworths emerged to challenge it**.

April 3rd. A train fireman was killed and the driver was badly injured when **a train on the NSW Bathurst line fell into a cavity caused by rain**. The train was pulling wood and petrol, and **the vapour from the petrol ignited and exploded**. The fireman was trapped under the engine.

April 3rd. Tokyo. One passenger was killed and 53 were injured when **a truck carrying sulphuric acid collided with a tram car** in a main shopping street in Tokyo. Screaming passengers splashed and **soaked by acid fought to escape from the acid fumes** that made breathing difficult. Injuries from acid burns were very severe and left deep scars.

Floods in the NSW country town of Dubbo drove 30 **Aborigines away from their normal riverbank dwellings**, and they were directed by police to the local **showground. But the committee there refused them entry.** Their reason was that property in the Ground would be damaged, including **the wood from buildings would be used for camp fires**....

This news item opens up the **tragic plight of the Aborigines round the nation**, and the wide gulf that separated them from the whites. At about this time, news items such as this **started** to stir the conscience of the whites, but **the first serious signs of redress did not come for another decade.**

Electric lawn mowers were getting very popular, and were taming many unruly swards. **But they came at a cost. A dozen males had been killed this year round Australia** by running over the trailing cord or by an electrical leak to the chassis.

The war finished 5 years ago, and now **zoning for bread deliveries has just been ended** in most States. This system was introduced in the war, and provided that bakers delivering bread should be given **an exclusive area, and would service that**. No one else could deliver in that area, and the baker could not deliver outside it....

This gradually became unpopular with housewives as they fell out with their given baker, and as some bakers became more autocratic given they had a monopoly. Five years later, the system was now gone, and **housewives everywhere were saying "good riddance."**

JAPANESE INVASION

Early in April, Letters to the Herald erupted with comment on whether we should allow Japanese into this country again, either as visitors or as migrants. It started with a small note that seemed innocuous, and rambled over familiar topics. But **the sting was in the last few words**. These opened up a string of correspondence, which I have sampled below.

Letters, R McEnvoy. I have waited for an abler pen than mine to make a protest against the admission of any Japanese to this country even for a short visit, no matter who their guarantor. For years before the recent War, every Japanese visiting these shores carried a camera, and Australia was photographed from one end to the other. This was despite the protests of hundreds of citizens who could see further than men whose job it was to protect us from spies.

After the 1914-18 war, Germany was allowed to re-arm itself because impractical dreamers and meddlers in high places had their way and, as a direct result, Europe was drenched in blood twice in 25 years.

In WWII, thousands of Australians were murdered, tortured, and starved by the Japs, and as it is the ordinary man who does the fighting in any war, why not consult him or the relatives of those who have suffered at the hands of **this sub-human race**.

Letters, B Dooley, University of Sydney. At the very time when we remember the crucifixion of Our Lord, praying forgiveness for his torturers, there comes a letter of protest against the admission of any Japanese to this country.

Does the writer realise that the Japanese were brutal because they were heathen, and that Japanese Christians were horrified when they learned of these atrocities? The Christian faith changes the whole outlook of a Japanese.

Let us take every opportunity of cementing Christian fellowship among all nations of the earth; let us encourage the Christians of Japan, and help Australian missionaries who are working with them.

Letters, A Enderby. Mr McEnvoy's recent letter refers to the Japanese as sub-human.

I agree, so why not treat them as the sub-human race from which mankind originated, and admit a few exhibits at Taronga Park Zoo and nowhere else.

Letters, C Bean. The problem of receiving visitors after the recent War depends on whether it is, or is not, too soon to over-ride the feelings of some of those who were most deeply hurt by Japanese conduct.

But in settling this difficult question, do not let us blind ourselves with the fallacy that this is the conduct of a "sub-human" race. Not race, **but a pernicious military tradition was the cause of it**; and history shows that when, in militaristic outbursts, we discard our Christian traditions (which, despite atom bombs, is humane) English, American, French, Dutch, Spaniards, and **we ourselves and all other men, can commit enormities just as shocking.**

The rubbish about "race" and supermen and submen should have died with Hitler; and your correspondents who advocate a Christian solution are right from the viewpoints of history and science also. The immediate problem, **the admission of a Japanese visitor to-day** would help that solution in which lies the only hope for our children and those of other lands.

Dr Bean was well-known historian in Australia. After WWI, he had been commissioned by the Government to write the official history of that war. He was a generous contributor to the Letters sections of newspapers, and his comments were taken into consideration by all readers.

Letters, R West. I sympathise with Dr Bean and others in their well-meaning but misguided efforts to convince fellow Australians that the time may have arrived to forgive and forget the behaviour of the Japanese troops in the last War.

Particularly do I feel sorry for Dr Bean, as his personal views are not founded on facts. As a historian, Dr Bean must be well aware that there always have been (and probably always will be) sub-human races, just as there always have been sub-human individuals.

Dr Bean says that the brutal behaviour of the Japanese, from high-ranking officers down to the humblest private, was due not to race, but to a "pernicious military tradition." He may not have seen first-hand evidence of Japanese bestiality, but those of us who did are not likely to subscribe to his views.

Would Dr Bean seriously suggest that the killing and eating of Australian soldiers, the disemboweling of pregnant women, and the staking out and raping of children were the result of military tradition? Would he say, too, that the pleasure taken by the Japanese in torturing dumb animals was produced by the same pernicious tradition?

I leave to the judgement of your readers Dr Bean's statement that "we ourselves can commit enormities just as shocking."

Letters, D Candisii. Brian Dooley praises Japanese Christians. I am only one of thousands who carry many scars from inhuman treatment and torture by so-called Japanese Christians.

Any ex-POW who worked on the Burma-Thailand Railway will tell you about Christian Japanese. I do not blame heathen Japanese for their treatment as they knew no better, but for the Christian and educated Japanese, I can see no excuse.

It would do well for writers to your columns to write of practical experience about the Japanese, not of theory and hearsay. Any Japanese will beg forgiveness and then knife you in the back.

Letters, Dr C Bean. I don't for a moment deny these cruelties. Indeed, I doubt that if we shall ever hear the worst of them. What I do say is that they are not due to distinctive "racial" characteristics, but to a pernicious militaristic tradition.

As a historian I know that the theory of racial sub- and super-men, as applied to any great nation today, is dangerous trash.

The ugly history of war proves that other races, **including our own**, **can**, even in modern times, **be guilty of enormities as great** in degree, if not in extent, **as those cited by Mr West**, and no one can claim that we have racially changed since their commission.

What has happened is that **we generally adhered, except in militaristic outbursts, to a humane Christian tradition.**

Letters, W Fisher, Eighth Division, Sydney. Dr Bean's contributions suggesting that the Japanese atrocities were on the same footing as the misdeeds of any army in any war, constitute such a misconception from a respected source that it is desired to express the different attitude of the 8th Division Council, of which I am President.

A reasonable people will agree that ultimate peace must entail the entry of Japan to a community of nations. Ex-prisoners of war, who in general are not vindictive, will agree with this. However, they will not in general agree that the necessary change of heart can have taken place in five short years.

Unlike travellers, diplomats, combat troops, occupation forces, prelates and General Mc Arthur himself, **they** had the unique experience of being representatives of the white race at the mercy of the brown dwarf when he thought himself on top of the world. The heart of the Japanese genius **must still be considered barbarian by Western standards**.

This does not imply consideration of sub-humanity or racial superiority. No one appreciates better than prisoners-of-war such strong points of the Japanese as intelligence, fighting strength, and capacity for discipline. It means precisely what is implied in the phrase "barbarian by Western standards," which is what concerns us.

By all means, let us be Christian and forgive, as far as in us lies, but **let us not be foolhardy and forget too soon**. Otherwise we offer our recent enemy a chance of one more imitation – of the resurgence of Germany after 1918 under the guise of a buffer against Communism.

Comment. These Letters show the depth of bitterness still felt here against the Japanese in 1950. It was well-based on the cruelty and atrocities that the Japanese dished out to prisoners all through Asia and the Pacific. It is not at all surprising that people were slow to forget.

I add a paragraph from **my 1948 book** that describes my own attitude to this.

A personal note. I must admit, with some shame, that I hung on to my resentment of the Japanese for far too long. By 1970, I was working for a large Japanese multi-national company in Sydney, and for a few years I had been urged to visit my counterpart in Tokyo. Every time, however, I found an excuse not to go. But at last, I was cornered and went reluctantly.

It took about a minute on the ground there for the troglodyte in me to die. I saw a vibrant, happy, intelligent people just going about their business, and not at all interested in the War. As I moved about I realised that they, the ordinary people, hated war as much as we do, and just wanted to live their lives to the full. So, I woke up, and felt better. My big regret is that I was about the last Australian to do so.

One further comment. Note that explicit mentions of Christianity keep getting into many Letters.

THE RED DEAN IS HERE

In mid-April, the good and holy people of England were getting themselves into quite a lather because the Dean of Canterbury had begun to preach on matters that were not scriptural, but rather social. In fact, he had gone a little further, and had made some favourable references to some of the credos of socialism. To some of his flock, and many others of no flock, this was seen as the first step on a downward spiral to Communism and, inevitably one small step further, to the end of civilisation as we know it. So, in the best democratic tradition, he was branded as a Communist sympathiser, and given the honorary title of the Red Dean.

This gentleman, Dr Hewlett Johnson, was now to visit Australia, and this in turn caused a commotion here. Remember that we too were at the start of a serious inquisition against Communism, compliments of the new Prime Minister Menzies, and this Red Dean visit provided a splendid opportunity for all the Red-baiters to further their cause. So, for the month of his visit, we were entertained by the Circus of the Year.

The first act was for the Sydney City Council **to refuse him the use of the Town Hall for a lecture**. This brought forth a salvo of Letters, some **for** the Archbishop, and some **against**. In any case, the battle lines were drawn.

Letters, A Phillis. The report that the City Council has, for political reasons, banned the use of the Town Hall for a meeting to be addressed by the Dean of Canterbury, must raise a real question in many minds.

The Council must, of course, have some discretion in these matters. But I believe that, by usage and on principles of civil liberty, persons of standing whom citizens may wish to hear on matters of importance, **should not be banned** from the facilities of the Town Hall. And, further, that **it is improper for the Council to assume the role of pre-censor of lawful public meetings, especially in the Town Hall.**

I dissent strongly from his reported views. But I support his right to express them publicly. Freedom cannot be switched on and off like an electric light, lest it too, suffer in total blackout.

Letters, Peter Howe. As a Protestant churchman, and a loyal subject of his Majesty King George VI, I would like to know by what right the Lord Mayor Alderman O'Dea and his City Council deny to the citizens of a British community the right to hear the Dean of Canterbury in Sydney Town Hall.

I remember well how Catholic Monsignor Fulton Sheen visited this city and affronted my beliefs and loyalties by a provocative speech on "Moscow or Rome." This gentleman was **not** denied the right to speak in the city's civic centre. Yet an eminent churchman like the

Dean of Canterbury, whose cathedral and in whose presence the beloved members of our Royal family often join in worship, is affronted by a clique of local party politicians.

I am in disagreement with the Dean's political views, but that is no reason why he should be denied the right to expound them.

Why, indeed, was the Dean refused when an equivalent Catholic with a somewhat similar message was approved? After all, they were both at times drawing attention to some similarities between Christianity and the theory of Communism. Both of these, **as philosophies**, were intent on sharing the wealth, and in helping the lot of the poor. But the Dean went further than that, and was much different from Sheen, in approving of the **political** system as practised in Russia. He had come out to Australia to attend a Peace rally that was simply a front for international Communism, and it was quite clear that this eminent churchman was ready to give Russia a mighty plug.

There were a lot of political figures who weren't keen on this. Hence the decision to refuse the use of the Town Hall. But there were other considerations, such as those raised above about the restraints on free speech. And there was the vexatious issue of similarities in the **philosophies** of Christianity and Communism. This latter matter took up many column-inches in the newspapers, with Letters that were generally so erudite that they were incomprehensible. I reproduce a few of these below, and perhaps you can get something out of them.

Letters, W Julian. The Dean said **he was Communist** in the classical definition of the word, **"as were all true**

Christians," but added that he did not belong to any political Party.

What is the classical definition of the word Communist? If the Dean wishes that we consider Acts 2:44,45, "and all that believed were together, and had all things common and parted them to all as every man had need," as the classical meaning, I agree that the ideal is wonderful, but I know of no group of people that are doing this at the present time.

The Dean should not couple such an ideal with the Russian form of Communism. The first qualification required for membership in the group spoken of in Acts was that he believed that Jesus was the Christ, the Son of the living God, the Saviour of men.

Can the Dean name one Communist, as the public understands the word, who has any desire to be associated with Christians.

Letters, E Suttor. Mr Julian asks "What is classical Communism?" I should answer by saying that the Dean meant by this term a summation of the social teaching of Jesus as the Master Himself expounds it in the Sermon on the Mount and other passages in the Synoptic Gospels.

Unfortunately, the interpretations of Scripture by sacerdotalism cannot always be relied upon. But if any man can read through the social teaching of the Synoptic Gospels and still call himself a Christian, while making no serious attempt to translate Christian precept into social practices along the lines therein indicated, I fail to see how such a person can claim the benefits of discipleship.

Whatever may be thought by the vested interests of Western civilisation, either commercial or clerical, of the great social experiment now being carried out in Russia, **I could never picture Christ opposing the**

efforts of those who would bring better conditions to the poor and oppressed. But I can readily envisage Him sternly rebuking mammonism in whatever disguise it might assume.

Letters, Arnold King, Dean of Goulburn.   When in England recently I had the privilege of visiting Canterbury. It was a proud moment when I stood within the walls of the great Cathedral, so worthy to be Mother Church of the Anglican Congregation.

From there, shortly, will come the Dean, a priest of the Church of England, who, to my knowledge, has never preached contrary to the plain teaching of scripture. An undemocratic and un-Australian reception is being prepared for him against which all true members of the Church of England should protest.

Last night the executive of the Anglican Men's Society, none of whom is a Communist nor am I, asked me to consent to an invitation being extended to the Dean to address the members. I gave that consent. Moreover, if the Dean is able to come to Goulburn, I shall invite him to preach at the Cathedral.

News Item, Sydney Airport.   The Red Dean said at the airport last night that he believed China was better off under a Communist regime. He rejoiced that the bloodshed had stopped, and he believed that a new order could replace the old one there. He was asked about his 1935 pronouncement that Canada and Australia should admit Japanese. He said that, at the time, that attitude was right, because it was a dog-in-the-manger approach that allowed white men in . and specifically excluded Asians.

Now these countries were admitting many migrants, of all colours. As an **aside** he went on to say **it is ridiculous to say that something said in 1935 should be considered**

to last forever. "Everyone should change their mind as their knowledge grows."

Meanwhile, the Red Dean had his share of social engagements, and managed to stay in the forefront of the news. At the Peace Conference in the Exhibition Hall in Melbourne, he was roundly cheered by 10,000 Communists, when he said that it was a lie that priests were persecuted in Russia. He went on to deny the claims that there was no morality in Russia, and that millions of people were in concentration camps there. More cheers. He emphasised that "it is the fashion of the millionaire Press to tell all kinds of lies about the Soviet people."

He painted a rosy picture of life in Russia. He said he had recently toured there, and had gone where-ever he pleased. He had never seen one sight that he wouldn't have liked a 17-year-old schoolgirl to see. The cost of living there was falling, and **the Soviet was universally seeking peace**.

There was a lot more cheering, but a request for a sponsor to fund his trip back to Britain fell on deaf ears, though a collection from the mass of people there netted 2,000 Pounds, which was more than enough for the purpose.

One young man was persistently shouting "Go home to Russia" when a woman slapped his face. He was then shouldered by another man and he lurched into another woman who almost fell over. The woman's husband then punched him in the ear and he was soon escorted from the pack by police.

A shower of coins was thrown onto the stage. Two of them hit the Dean and a request was issued to stop. It took several minutes for this request to filter through.

On leaving Australia, the US government refused him entry. When he departed Australia, he left his mark through his dozens and dozens of public appearances, and he probably went from the nation with a few more friends than when he arrived. He got them, though, not so much because of his message, but because of his effusive, infectious, good-natured presentation of his cause that seemed to offer some hope of co-operation with the Reds, rather than direct head-on confrontation.

In any case, I leave you make the final decision. Which of these two writers is nearer the truth?

Letters, John Baalman. Dr Hewlett Johnson is right when he says Russia does not want war.

What Russia wants is conquest. Preferably peaceful conquest. The same could have been said of Hitler. But the alternative is war, if you can't get peaceful conquest.

But Hitler did not use so many clerical dupes in his plan as Russia does. In America, they call them suckers.

Letters, O Hazelwood. As an English-born Christian of the younger generation, I feel bound to express my deep gratitude to the Dean of Canterbury for the privileged opportunity of hearing his inspiring address preached from the pulpit of St Andrews Cathedral last Sunday evening. Could the youth of Australia have listened as I did to the Red Dean, and seen in his eyes the very symbols of love, peace and wisdom, they would have felt that at least one man was striving constructively for world peace.

This was no illusion, nor was it the thought of a fanatical Communist, but only of a peace-loving conservative English Christian.

MAY NEWS ITEMS

The Federal Government is toying with the idea of **starting a national health insurance scheme for all eligible citizens**. This would require persons to join a fund, and thereafter be covered for a large part of their health costs. Those who did not join would struggle on by themselves.....

Sounds familiar? That is much the same as we take for granted now. But in **those days it was very controversial,** with everyone having a reason why it would not work, and **why they would be dudded by the scheme....**

Still, with lots of different approaches over the many years, and lots of perennial complaints over the levels of premiums, **it is now working pretty well** in Australia, and there would be many people unhappy if it went away or was changed much.

The Northern Territory has employed two doggers for the first time. The State is confronted with a dingo problem of major proportions, and have employed two men to reduce this menace. **They will not use rifles** and bullets, because it causes too much suffering to animals if they are just wounded....

Instead, they will **use poison and bait, and these presumably are painless**. They will be paid a salary, with camping allowance, and **a bonus of one Pound for each scalp presented**. One Dogger said that if he got one hundred scalps in the first week, and if he could maintain that, **he would "earn a fortune."**

A Royal Commission in London has brought forth claims, by eminent scientists, that continuing **economic pressures discourage high intelligence individuals from breeding**, and so those with low intelligence will grow to be dominant. It estimated that 65 per cent of Britain's population would be of sub-standard intelligence **by the year 2000**. **"Feeble-mindedness would increase from 1.5 per cent to 4.1 per cent."**

England now had a glut of dairy products, and **our cream was no longer necessary for making British butter**. So now, whacko, **the Government's ban on the sale of cream in Australia was lifted.** Those wonderful scones with strawberry jam and cream will be back, and Mums can again spend their Sunday mornings making pavlova for **the Sunday dinner**.

The Speaker in the House of Representatives came across a group of six journalists playing **threepenny poker in the Press Room**. He made a statement to the House. **"I will not tolerate gambling in any form.** If a player is a Press man, I will remove his accreditation. If he is an employee, I will sack him. If he is a Member, I will report him to the House for censure...."

All Australians were of course thrilled that they had such a vigilant Speaker looking after their morals.

Those of you who have **ice chests** had better stock up. The price of ice will rise seven per cent for **a full block** on Monday, and ten percent for **a half block**.

Remember that if you took ice deliveries, they were always delivered door-to-door by **an ice-man**.

THE RED MENACE

On April 28th, Prime Minister Menzies proposed to Parliament that laws should be enacted that would impose severe restraints on all Communist activities in Australia. During the election campaign at the end of 1949, he had made it clear that his Government would launch an all-out attack on Communism, and this proposed Bill did just that.

The Bill provided that the Communist Party should be dissolved, and all of its property and assets should be confiscated. Also, that all affiliated organisations, such as Youth Leagues, would be declared unlawful. It went on to state that persons who had been Communists after May 1948, and who might be considered prejudicial to the nation's security, may be "declared." This meant that they would not be eligible for employment by the Commonwealth or occupy any Trade Union office.

It was clear that, in the Bill, any Communist who contributed to strike action would be acting in a manner "prejudicial to the nation's security". And it was clear that people even remotely associated with Communism, or with Communist-controlled Trade Unions, were likely to be drawn into the sorry business of having to defend their actions in Court.

One very contentious clause of the Bill required that the onus of proof be placed on the defendant. In other words, if a person was **accused** of being a Communist, or a sympathiser, and it was argued that he could be acting contrary to the nation's interest, it was up to him **to prove to a Court that he was not thus involved**. Of course, this was against the popular understanding of British justice, which generally held that a person was innocent until proven guilty.

Opposition to the Bill was widespread, and so too was support for it. This small sample, taken from hundreds of Letters actually published by newspapers across the nation, gives you some idea of the arguments.

Letters, 1702 Sgt. 10ᵗʰ Btn, 1ˢᵗ AIF. It seems to me that Mr Menzies could go a step further in the direction of putting the Communists in their proper places. Besides outlawing the Party, and removing individual members from Government and Trade Union office, the following additional moves might be undertaken.

Firstly. Any known Communist should be debarred from **owning any property**, and his present holdings to be confiscated and the proceeds from the sale to be placed to the credit of defence funds. **Secondly,** all civil rights to be withheld from any known Communist.

Thirdly. All travel for Communists to be on the same basis as alien travel permits in war-time, namely, reporting to the police at every town and obtaining authority to move to another town.

In other words, these holders of ideas so alien to our Australian way of life should be given only just so much freedom as any ordinary Australian would be permitted if allowed into Russia.

Letters, F Coss. In view of the damning evidence that the Prime Minister gave in support of the Bill, one **would have expected the Communist spokesperson to have defended his Party** against the withering attack made upon it. On the contrary, he did not even deny the allegations that his party is subversive and revolutionary, pledged to overthrow of constitutional government by violence. By his failure to deny the allegations, he has tacitly admitted that they are true.

He endeavours to conceal the real issue by appealing to the Australian sense of fair play, and by calling for the support of Trade Unionists in the fight to preserve the right of unionists to elect the officials they desire.

It is to be hoped that decent Trade Unionists will not be duped again by the comrades' glibness. Unctuous references to the principles of British justice by those who are pledged to undermine it are, in the words of Mr Menzies, "arrant humbug."

Letters, Colin Rose. "Thank God for Mr Menzies" should be the cry of every decent Australian today. Here at last we have a Prime Minister, trained in law, and determined to obliterate entirely a Party shrewd in the practice of circumventing the law. He is the first political leader in the world to publicly proscribe the Communists and move constitutionally to ban their wretched existence.

If the Senate causes another election on this issue, it will sound the death knell of the Labor Party, which on this occasion cannot run with the hare and hunt with the hounds.

Letters, Christian Social Order Program, Sydney. Among the many obnoxious traits of Communists, which have turned Australians against them, is their habit of tearing to shreds the private and political reputation of those who oppose their line, and their shrill yelling of "Fascist" against those who insist on holding orthodox opinions.

Still, it would be a colossal tragedy if Australians were now misled by their hostility to Communists into permitting **the same sort of malicious and suppressive tactics** from the Menzies extremists on "the right."

That such extremists exist, some of them in Parliament, and that they are already taking advantage of proposals of the anti-Communist Bill to hang the label "Red" around the necks of persons and groups who remain critical of Capitalism and imperialism.

There are many scathing critics of Communism who are far from satisfied that capitalist "democracy" and colonisation are free of injustice, inhumanity and denial of essential freedoms. It would be intolerable if such people were exposed to denunciation and falsely charged with Marxist ideology.

Many eyes and ears are turned towards the Prime Minister, awaiting the assurance that the strong measures proposed in the Bill will, after becoming law, never be allowed to be abused for the restriction or curtailment of essential liberty of thought, opinion, assembly, and expression.

Letters, Lloyd Ross.   Britain is much more in danger of sudden destruction, and is suffering from industrial unrest, but it has not banned the Communist Party.

Circumstances no doubt alter cases, but the main thing in Britain is the existence in Britain of a traditional belief in the importance of individual freedom which, unfortunately in Australia, has come to be regarded as being irrelevant on many issues of freedom.

In the present discussion on the Bill are a basic error and a fallacy. The **error** is the belief that **industrial unrest will be removed by the elimination of Communist interference**.

This means that one cannot defend the right of individuals to express their opinions without being identified with the principles themselves.

It's time we took down from our shelves such books as John Stuart Mills' on "Liberty", and tested the present legislation by a classical statement of the defence of the liberty of the individual.

Letters, Briton.   Never in any British country has any citizen had the right to preach treason; nor have traitors possessed the right of free assembly.

In more virile times, treasonable utterances and assemblies were punishable by death.

Letters, A MINER, Cessnock.   I am a member of a Communist-sponsored Youth League. Lots of young men get together and play sport every week-end of the year. We get no political indoctrination at all. We play with this club because the others in society, like the Churches, are too smug and lazy to help us form other teams and Associations.

The "Communists" who run the league have no interest in Russian Communism. They believe in socialism, more so than the Labor men, but not too much more. The whole idea of some sort of revolution and all that nonsense has no interest for them. They want a better world where the wealth does not **all** go to people like Barron Brown.

When this Bill passes, every one of these men can be declared. Probably I can too. All because Menzies wants to scare the dupes of the nation into thinking that there is some sort of crisis on hand. I bet he doesn't believe it himself, but he does a good job of convincing other foolish people.

Finally, it's a disgrace that I am forced to write to a paper using a pen-name. I know it probably won't work anyway, because the "spies" will have the power to have access to the newspapers' record. What sort of a country are we becoming?

The proposed legislation left the Labor Party on the horns of a dilemna. **Firstly**, most Trade Unions opposed it, as you might expect, and those that were Communist dominated were **bitterly** opposed. **Secondly**, many opposed it on the basis that free speech and the right of association would be denied, and that the banning of a political Party was completely outside the ambit of Australian democratic thinking. **Thirdly**, they were worried that the Government would use the new law to harass the Labor Party.

But Labor was on dangerous ground, as a political Party. There could be no doubt that if they opposed the Bill, they would be branded as Communist **fellow-travellers**. That is, as sympathisers, with one foot in the Communist camp. The entire Western world was on a witch hunt against Communist influence; remember that Joe McCarthy in the USA was getting all the headlines for his purge over there. Here, it would have been suicide for Labor to oppose the Bill, and so, they reluctantly said they would support it in both Houses of Parliament.

But, they sought to **amend** it in a few ways. They made most headway in this by shooting at the "onus of proof" provision. Surely, they said, it was outside all concept of British justice that a person should be declared guilty until he could prove his own innocence. They pounded away at this provision, but Menzies was adamant. He argued that the time that elapsed in Court cases would otherwise take too long, and by the time a decision could be made, the damage (whatever that was) would be done.

He argued that, if the Government had to prove its case, then it would have to reveal where it got its information from, and that would diminish the effectiveness of its sources. So the proposition became that "spies" could provide information that could have the person declared, this information would not need to be revealed, nor would the informant be liable for questioning. Clearly this was a worry for all opponents of the Government. What would stop it from simply inventing a spy, and declaring an opponent? Then leave that person with the difficult task of proving he was not subversive.

So allegations flew backwards and forwards for a month of bitterness. Then Menzies, with the Bill scarcely changed, put it to Parliament. He had the majority in the Lower House, and it passed easily. In the Senate, Labor still had a majority, left over from the previous election, and they did their best to delay the passage. They won some amendments, so the Bill was sent back to the House for their approval again. But after a few weeks of manoeuvering, Menzies said that the amended Bill would, if passed, no longer serve its initial purpose, and he withdrew it for the moment and **would re-present it in three months.**

Menzies' big stick. At this stage, I will remind readers that Menzies, as a Liberal, had control of the more important Lower House, and he used it to initiate legislation all the time. But the Upper House, or Senate, had to review the Bills presented to it, and could reject them if it thought it wise. Menzies was thus in constant danger of having a favoured Bill rejected.

The solution to this threat for Menzies was to actually have that happen, and then convince the Governor General that he was being frustrated in the business of governing by a hostile Senate, and **ask for a double dissolution**. This meant that both Houses of Parliament would be fully dissolved, and that new elections would be held to fill the two Houses.

Menzies had a pretty good idea that if this happened now, at the time of the anti-Communist Bill, he would win comfortably in both Houses. So, he was quite sanguine about the passage of it in the Senate. **If it failed** there, then he would seek a double dissolution. **If it passed**, he would be happy to have won through, and he could certainly find cause for a double dissolution over the next important issue.

So, at this stage, Menzies shrugged his shoulders, and virtually said "I'll see you in three months when I re-introduce the Bill." It was a definite threat. **The Bill would be passed then, or he would go for a double dissolution.** And that would mean that many sitting Labor members would lose their seats. And so, **to close this story for a short while**, I report that Mr Menzies then pulled up stumps and went to Britain, and other countries, for a period of – you guessed it – three months.

Let me make three points before changing topic.

Firstly, the newspapers were absolutely full of coverage of these events. About 25 per cent of the first four pages of every metropolitan daily for a month was taken up with them. It was the story of the year.

Secondly, all other nations of the Western world were fascinated by our "adventure". They saw Australia as a brave, or perhaps foolish, pioneer in the battle against Communism. So their newspapers and officials were rich in free advice on how right, or how wrong it all was, and how we should do it. In the long run, though, no other nation tried to emulate us, and we remained a pioneer without any settlers behind us.

Thirdly, most commentators agree that the real purpose behind the Bill was to reduce the number of strikes that the nation suffered. Chifley, the year before, had done this in the miners' strike by freezing the funds of the miners, and starving them back to work. Menzies now had a different approach. When he talked about **violating national security, he really meant calling a strike,** or advocating a strike. In the course of Parliamentary debate, he had presented to Parliament a list of the names of 53 persons he would declare, and all of these were leaders of Communist-led Trade Unions. Menzies in fact was seriously embarrassed by this a few days later, when he had to admit that four of the persons on the list were completely innocent of any involvement at all. It seemed to make a mockery of his repeated assurances that his policies would be exercised with the maximum of fairness and restraint. But in any case, this was just a slight hiccup, and he went ahead without any qualms.

MOTHERS' DAY SENTIMENTS

Letters, M Constance Cook.   Mother's Day will be here again soon, with all the usual impediments – white flowers, slippers, sugar basins, and sentiment.

Some of us regard this day unfavourably, and have requested our children to ignore it. We feel that we are, above all else, rational human beings, then mothers. Also, that having taken it upon ourselves to bring our children here without their knowledge or consent, the most we can do for them is at times the least. No sensible mother wishes to be idealised nor to burden her children with an uneasy sense of obligation.

Any woman who has known the spontaneous, trustful, pure love of a child has been amply rewarded, and if this precious spark can be kept glowing through the years there is no need for lip-service and cheap outwardly trappings.

If homage must be paid to women on one day of the year, let it be extended to include all those others, scholars and humanitarians, who devote themselves to the welfare of other people's children – teachers, social workers, nurses, kindergarten experts, and all who give of themselves in service. The mere producing of children calls for no intelligence, whereas their training and education demand infinite care and wisdom.

It is noticeable that Father's Day has never been very successful. No doubt it makes the average man feel slightly ridiculous – and here one pays tribute to his superior sense of humour.

All this Mother's Day sentimentality (whipped up largely by commercial interests) lowers woman's dignity and retards her cause.

Letters, M Grace Darby.   I am heartily in accord with Constance Cooke. About 1909, my father, the late Reuben Bailey, learning of its organisation in America by Miss Jarvis, introduced Mother's Day to his congregation in Fremantle. In those days, there was no commercialisation of the movement. We were urged to express our appreciation to our mother, by spoken word or letter.

Mother's Day is a reminder to express something of our love and appreciation. The wearing of the white flower is the outward sign of the love and reverence felt for motherhood.

JUNE NEWS ITEMS

Australia was a long way from the trouble spots in the world. Our newspapers were full of reports of hassles in Germany, of sulky petty arguments with Russia, and of the posturing of MacArthur in Japan. But **we here shrugged it all off**, and worried about things that we could do something about....

The world was pressing us to get more involved. **Things were building up overseas.** We now agreed to **send planes to Malaya** to help the Brits suppress the Reds. **The price of wool was sky-rocketing**, indicating that someone was buying. For what purpose? It had to be for **keeping a lot of soldiers warm in freezing climates. Where could that be?**

The **world leader of the Salvation Army** left Australia after a seven-week tour. He observed that there was **more drunkeness in Australia** that "in any other place I have been to".

There are "billions" of Argentine ants in Perth and Melbourne already, and now they are s**preading to Sydney**. The only known eradicant is DDT mixed in with kerosene in a bait of syrup. But that only protects the area it is laid on. The brown ants, less than a tenth of an inch long, **eat everything voraciously**, and the ground in some Melbourne suburbs is "literally" alive with them.

June 25. North Korea invaded South Korea with tanks and artillery at 11 points along their common border. It is too early to know if this is just a border incident and if the northerners will retire after making a point....

But it is known that the US is moving ships and manpower and supplies to the region, and that does not suggest a peaceful outcome.

The *SMH* promises that next Sunday will be a special day. It will publish a 28-page Brides Supplement, lavishly illustrated, with pictures and designs for bridal frocks, going-away clothes, and the trousseau generally. There will also be special sections dealing with etiquette, bouquets, wedding procedure, and the planning and furnishing of the first home.

A motor cyclist in Sydney's Redfern hit a pedestrian who was knocked to the ground, but **got his foot caught in the bike**. The bike remained upright and dragged him 50 yards until it hit a car. Then it started **to spin in a circle for two minutes, still dragging the man.** Eventually it ran into another parked car and stopped. The pedestrian was taken to hospital but **he died soon after arrival**. He was 82 years of age.

In the Queen's Birthday Honours list, **General Blamey was commissioned as Field Marshall**. He was the first Australian to be appointed to this position. He had an interesting career between the wars, and was Victorian Commissioner of Police for much of that time. As **the Commander of Australian forces during the war**, he was much respected by many military men, though he had quite a few detractors.

TRIALS OF WAR CRIMINALS

Five years after the Wars were over, the US started the trials of major war criminals in Los Negros, one of the so-called New Guinea Islands. A few years earlier, Australia had conducted its own trials at a number of Malayan and Pacific locations, and had somewhat laid to rest many of the great tragedies that had befallen our troops. In 1950, America finally brought to trial some of the military personnel who **it** considered to be major war criminals, like General Tojo; though **Emperor** Hirohito was spared the ordeal of prosecution due to the intervention of MacArthur. Many of the servicemen who had suffered at the hands of Japanese were Australian, and some of these were called upon to testify at Los Negros.

Comment.   Right now, I am undecided about how to proceed here. On the one hand, I covered a little of the Australian war trials in earlier books in this Series. So now, apart from not wanting to repeat myself, I also want to avoid stirring up matters that will remind many people of things they would perhaps want to forget, or to remember only in times of their own choosing. On the other hand, these trials were important events in 1950, so I could hardly justify not making mention of them .

What I have done is report below the testimony given by one Australian soldier in an affidavit at the trials. Here he recounts some of the atrocities experienced by himself and his colleagues, but he does not, of course, go on to describe the other terrible things done to others.

Additional comment.   I am still unhappy about recording this evidence here. It is now about 70 years since the War ended, and **in a conversational book of this type,** I do not want to open up old wounds. And on top of that, the Japanese people now are our good friends, so why would I persist in dragging the worst of their history into the open? The only answer I can offer is, to repeat, the trials happened in 1950, and simply must be reported.

Lieutenant Ben Hackney, of Bathurst NSW. Lt Hackney described the last hours of 110 Australian and 35 Indian troops whom Japanese soldiers massacred in Malaya in January, 1942. His testimony was given at the trial of Lieut-General Nishimura and his aide, Nonaka, who were held to be responsible for the executions. This evidence, slightly edited for brevity, is given below.

About 2.30 p.m. on January 22nd all enemy fire ceased. Shortly afterwards, Japanese soldiers closed in on our position. With much unintelligible yelling, they indicated that we had to assemble at a point west of the road.

Some of the fit men, who were very few, were allowed to help the more unfortunate. The others were compelled to move to the assembly area and remain. Assembly was slow, men incapable of movement lying all over the place. There were about 110 Australians and 35 Indians. Then the prisoners were forced into a small house, and even the dead were taken inside.

An Indian soldier who had been knocked down in front of the building was showing signs of regaining consciousness. He began to sit up, but the Jap in charge kicked him over again. While the Indian lay still, groaning, the Jap stuck a bayonet into him again and again. Nishimura then issued his orders about what was to be done with the prisoners.

About sunset, guards began to move about the hut. Machine-guns were placed in front of the building. The prisoner officers were then tied together with the following method. The officers were made to stand while both hands were tied behind his back tightly with rope. After this, another length of rope was tied to the wrists, passed up and under the chin and down again to the wrists, where it was pulled tight, thus forcing the hands well up the back and making the rope terribly tight against the throat.

A second rope was then passed to the wrists of the next officer, then to the next, and so on, so that as well as being tightly bound, the officers were all linked together. The other ranks were then brought from the rooms, tied brutally with their hands behind their backs, then one was joined to the other from wrists to wrists. The supply of rope ran out and some Japs brought pieces of wire with which they tied many prisoners. Nearly every man was lashed about the head and kicked. Often a soldier who was difficult to tie because of his wounds was subjected to lashings, sometimes with wire, and kicked. Occasionally, another guard seeing his fellow soldier beating a prisoner would rush up and add to that soldier's misery by striking him with a rifle butt.

When the line of officers began to move off, one of them fell immediately. After being kicked on all parts of the body, and struck many times with rifle butts, he was cut free from the chain. I also fell after very little movement. The Japs became more annoyed, apparently because I was the second one to fall, and I suffered greater ill-treatment. One kick split my right eye-brow, which then hung down over my eye, blood pouring over my face.

The others were forced along, and I was dragged a short distance. Eventually the Japs cut me loose, and left me lying on the ground in a much worse and painful condition than before. The wound on my back had been kicked many times.

The prisoners were then marched off around the building. Many were unable to move at all and others, because they were tied, could not get the necessary assistance so that they stumbled and fell, causing others to fall. They were kicked, struck, and bayoneted until as many as could do so were standing again.

The prisoners were then herded into a group, and the massacre which followed was, to say the least, most violent and wicked.

Rifles and machine-guns belched forth a storm of death. A few fell, and then the group fell. After the first burst, a few remained standing, but they were hit by rifle or machine-gun fire. The firing was indiscriminate, and many then fell not because they were hit but because they were pulled down by others falling.

The Jap soldiers then returned to the front of the building and began taking away the bodies of those who had been cut free of the ropes to allow the progress of the line. These they dragged around a corner to where the others had been taken. They left behind only one body, this being the farthest away of the two officers who had been previously cut away from the chain. This was I.

My only hope of escape was to make the Japs believe me dead and, perhaps, stand a chance of being left lying there. I knew I should have appeared dead enough, provided I remained quite still. Blood was all over me, my hair was matted with blood and dirt, my back was still bleeding, and my right leg blood from the knee down. I lay quite still, very uncomfortable. The ropes cut off the circulation in my hands. My hands were still in the vicinity of my shoulder-blades.

Some Japs came and stood over me awhile and, as if to make sure, one pushed me several times with his boot. I allowed my body to move freely in the direction it was forced. Some of them kicked me, then left. Some Japs went to the road, leaving a few behind to fire in the direction of any sound or movement, and returned bearing many tins of petrol which were carried on our vehicles. They proceeded to pour this over the prisoners, many of whom were still conscious. The prisoners were then set alight.

I had managed to be dead as far as some of the Japs were concerned and now, more than ever, I was determined that no matter what pain I was suffering and how my body ached, I would remain dead. How many times I was kicked and battered with rifles I know not, but all the time I had to maintain a lifeless attitude.

For ages, the Japs maintained a patrol about the area, occasionally firing shots. Many times Japs passed my body, often satisfying themselves that I was dead by the previously used methods. Some used a bayonet, most just prickled me in the back. On two occasions they were more than pricks. Once a Jap jumped and pranced as he lunged at me, but fortunately he was too far away and the bayonet entered my side between the ribs and apparently did no harm. Once a bayonet struck my right elbow, making it useless for many days. One Jap decided that he would have my boots and caused me much pain while he pulled them off my feet.

Eventually there was no sign of activity in the area, but I waited long after this before being certain that no one was patrolling. I knew that to be seen moving would be the end.

Much later, after painfully forcing myself from my bonds, I crawled to the water and was met by an American sergeant and another soldier. Both smelt strongly of petrol. They had been with the group when fired upon and set alight. The sergeant told me that they were among the few who had not been tied. They had fallen – neither of them hit – when the first group was fired upon, and lay with the remainder. When the petrol was brought from the road, they both had some thrown on them. The sergeant got himself and the other man free from the group and lay still close by until the Japs left.

After spending 14 days lying in and crawling about the jungle and rubber plantations, I was captured by Malaya policemen and taken to Purit Selong police station on February 27, 1942.

Comment. In an earlier Chapter, Doctor Bean said in his letter that all soldiers, including Australians, were capable of atrocious behaviour at times under war conditions. Perhaps he is right; but I sincerely hope he is wrong.

Letters, H Finlay. I have just read Lt Hackney's evidence. It is impossible to imagine that more revolting cruelty could be inflicted by civilised men, than was that day given to our unfortunate soldiers who were prisoners of war in the hands of the Japanese.

While that evidence is being given, we will soon have in Australia a member of that depraved race to whom will be extended the privileges of dedicating the memorials which we are still erecting to honour those who perished by the brutality of his countrymen.

Could any greater indifference be shown to the justifiable feelings of our people.

BRITAIN'S RUGBY LEAGUE TOUR

Rugby League is a funny game. What happens is that two teams, each of thirteen players, go to the same field and tackle, and punch, and shove and maul each other for 80 minutes. There are all sorts of officials running round, some of them playing with whistles, and others with flags, and still others who carry the stretchers for those inevitably maimed. There is a ball or two thrown onto the field to act as a focal point for the violence, and often the whole frenzy is watched by packs of supporters who are remarkable in that each of them has only one eye.

As with all sporting teams, the best players gradually make their way to the top, and in League, this guarantees that when they play, the mayhem is sadistically satisfying. The very best players for Australia are put into a Test team, and the same is true for England, and every two or three years, the two Test teams do battle against each other in three Test matches, and the winner gets **bragging rights** until next time. Needless to say, they use those rights endlessly.

In Winter 1950, the English team toured Australia, playing games against local teams, and State teams, and ultimately against Australia. Most of the games were played in NSW and Queensland. League is not very popular in the other States, because the daily temperature is fairly low there. That means that the scorers do not wear thongs, and so when the scores get over 10 points, it all becomes too hard.

The build-up, in the Press, for the First Test was enormous. Many of the English players had already achieved the status of legends in the five years since the War ended. And in Australia, we too had our giants of the game. Local conditions were also great in that floods had devastated the Eastern coast of Australia, so the game was certain to be played on a mud-heap. Crowds were big, and country people were having great difficulty getting scarce city accommodation. Many slept out in the parks close to the Sydney Cricket Ground. Grog could be taken into the Ground in those days, and it looked like a big day for all is coming up.

The excitement was added to by the claims, made by English players and supporters, about the treatment that The Poms were getting on and off the fields. There were the inevitable stories that local referees were supporting home teams, which they certainly were. What else can a touring team expect, I hear some of you ask. There was this little plea in the Letters to the *SMH*.

Letters, COOGEE. Is it not high time that some action should be taken by either the Rugby League Football Committee or the Sydney Cricket Ground Trust to stop the booing of spectators when an English player is about to take a penalty kick.

This unfair practice has been allowed to go on for years in Australia, and I consider that something should be done to stop it. Surely we are sporty enough to give our visitors from the homeland a decent fair go.

Question. Did I hear someone saying something about pigs might soon learn to fly?

The First Test turned out to be a thriller, as was promised. The final score saw Australia lose 4 to 6, with just two goals versus two tries. It was an exciting match, though very hard for amateurs to follow, because after one minute, all players were covered from head-to-toe with a thick coating of mud from the cricket pitch at the SCG. Australia got close to equalling the score when Pidding tried for goal, and hit the cross-bar. One radio commentator said that a giant gust of wind blew the posts at an improper moment, and that the ball then had to travel one inch extra, and so missed. It was hard to verify that from the TV re-play, because there was no TV in those days.

The Second Test was more satisfactory for the Australians, because they won. The Poms complained that they were robbed, because two of their men were sent off in separate incidents. The Englishmen went on over the next few weeks to complain about the referees, and were appeased for the next Test by being given some say in the choice for the final Test. Needless to say, in the finest sporting tradition, all their complaints about the ref were a delight to Aussie ears, after all the complaints we had made in the previous tour of England two years earlier. Like I said, League is a funny game.

BARKING DOGS

Right now, in 2016, it's a bit hard to be a dog if you live in the cities or towns. Everything you used to like doing, back in 1950, is taboo. For example, can you run out onto the road, and bite a mailman on his bike on the ankle? Can you bail up a pack of terrified little school kids against a fence? Can you bark from go to whoa at any visitor who comes near your property? Can you even bark at night without getting a visit from the cops?

Can you roam the streets at will, fouling the area as you go? What about a good dog-fight with ten other sets of snarling teeth? None of these. They are all taboo. And what have the domesticates got in return? They spend all day locked inside a house, or a small back-yard. Every second day, someone grabs their leash, and pooper-scooper, and plastic bags, and takes them for a walk on the concrete footpaths and over the concrete driveways. If they see another dog they are dragged away, if they see a cat, they are dragged away, and they never see a rabbit. It's a dog' s life.

Back in 1950, things were a lot easier for dogs. But, as the following Letters show, things were starting to toughen up for dogs who barked at night.

Letters, ANTI-DOG, Artarmon.   It was reported recently in Milan that the city Administration of Milan, Italy, decided to increase the cost of dog licences from two Pounds to five Pounds. The reason was that dogs, which do not serve a useful purpose, must be regarded as taxable luxuries.

In our suburban areas when a person buys a dog, they also purchase the sleep and rest of their neighbours. These yelping and whining nuisances are apparently on the increase, and it is high time licences here were increased to say five Pounds. This might keep the number down, and at the same time provide a valuable source of revenue for the State.

Letters, INSOMNIA. I sincerely hope Anti-Dog's letter will call forth wide public feeling against a nuisance that is causing endless trouble amongst neighbours and considerable ill-health due to loss of sleep.

Local health inspectors are hesitant about acting, and if a private person asks the Court to abate the nuisance, it is likely to cost him some money, and the harmony of the neighbourhood, and the dogs still bark at night.

Barking dogs have sent me to the psychiatrist, and my wife into the country in search of peaceful slumber.

Letters, S Lacey. May I suggest that Anti-Dog purchase a dog himself. Apparently he has never had a dear trusting face to welcome him home, has never looked into those great big eyes and been stirred by the trust and affection so obvious in them, or been licked most generously by a little red tongue.

Perhaps if he sees the owner of the offending dog and suggests tactfully **the use of a fine leather strap** when these nightly attacks occur, it will not be long before he is having undisturbed rest.

Letters, M Neitenstein. About those barking dogs. A dog that is properly fed and that has shelter to sleep in, will not bark at night. A dog wants to sleep and if he barks, he cannot rest, he is hungry and cold. He is begging for help in the only way he can.

The use of the strap, as suggested, is not the remedy. What is required is a little kindness and common sense and a suggestion to the owner that the poor animal is in misery these cold and wet nights.

Letters, Fuzzy, Sydney University. In Port Moresby, we eat dogs that bark at night. We also eat dogs that don't. They taste like lamb. My grandfather tells me that they are not as nice as the white men he used to eat when he was up the jungle.

Letters, D Morgan. While there are hard-bitten dealers catering for the likely sentimental people who drool over pups one day and, having obtained them, neglect them the next, there will always be too many dogs on the streets ill-cared for and badly trained.

But why blame the "yelping and whining nuisances" when, with a little kindness and understanding, they can be God's gift to lonely and unhappy people and certainly no trouble to their neighbours.

Put the blame where it is due, and not on poor dumb animals who cannot reply in their own self defence.

Letters, LONG-SUFFERING NEIGHBOUR. Your correspondents write of barking dogs. But what of screaming babies. I have had to put up with this annoyance for 10 years from my inconsiderate next-door neighbours.

This kind of thing goes on all day, and well past midnight, without the parents seeking the trouble. I consider this menace is more nerve-wracking than that of barking dogs. Or is one as bad as the other?

NEWS AND VIEWS

Princess Margaret growing up. Margaret was now of the age when young men were hanging about and trying to look indifferent. She, for her part, was being a bit difficult, and not quite playing the game. That is, she did not seem to be attached to any particular suitor, and, had she been anyone else, might have been described as "playing the field."

The long wait is over. It was announced at the end of June that rationing of butter and tea would cease immediately. There had been many dour predictions that when this happened there would be such a rush that all the shops would be left without supplies for a month. But as it turned out, shoppers were quite sensible about this, and no such rush occurred.

Comment. I am still amazed that butter here was rationed five years after the War ended. I know that Britain wanted and got a lot of our butter, and that the War had decreased our capacity to produce. And I know of a few other reasons. But I do not accept it was still necessary to ration it for all of the last five years, and that it took a new government to get the new system in place. Somehow, somewhere, there was a great deal of cupidity, to say the least. **The regulators from the war years** hung in there for a long time.

JULY NEWS ITEMS

A 43-year-old **woman fell from the top of the Gap** in Sydney. This is a cliff at the entrance to the Harbour where people go to see the view. It is also much used by intending suicides who throw themselves off the top. **There is a drop of 175 yards to the rocks below** at low tide....

This woman slipped and fell the full distance. As she landed, **a giant wave came in and she slid down the face of it,** and ended up burbling about in a lot of water. **She suffered only slight abdominal injuries,** and was released from hospital after a short period of rest and close observation.

The English Rugby League team was touring Australia. There had been the usual biffs on the field, and harsh words said by officials off the field. It was, then, **a completely normal tour**....

But, press reports from Queensland said that the Brits were so hated in Brisbane that **they were not brave enough to wear their blazers in public.** This story circulated for a few days, and as usual gained momentum as time passed....

But it was quashed when team management pointed out that **the blazers had all been handed in for scheduled dry-cleaning.** "We have nothing but the greatest respect for Queenslanders, and I know they feel the same toward us." It is just that, in the true spirit of sportsmen world-wide, Australians simply hated the other team. Not the individual.

The situation in Korea has deteriorated badly,and 15,000 youths will be called up as soon as practical for compulsory military service.

Comment. This was of particular interest to me because **I was one of the lucky ones** who made it into the early batches.

The executives of the Seaman's Union are heading for hot water. They are almost all Communists, and support the Reds in Korea. They decided that ships leaving Australian ports **would not carry arms and food for our troops** now fighting there....

There is national outrage at this, and the rank and file seamen also oppose this decision. So too does an angry Government. **That executive had better back down quickly or things might get tough.**

Sydney established a record one day this week. Every single suburb had a serious blackout, lasting for an average of two hours. This was because of breakdown at every station in the grid. That takes a lot of organising.

The Cabinet has decided **to prosecute the Seamens' Union under the Crimes Act.** This Act is applied only to very serious situations, and **carries severe penalties on those convicted.** It is the **Government's Big Stick, rarely used, but always effective. The Cabinet have the support of almost all the nation**, including the vast majority of trade unionists. **Will the Seamens' Union crack in the face of this?**

KOREAN WAR STARTS

At the end of WWII, the United States was the military occupant of South Korea, while Russia was occupying the North. Under a United Nations scheme, the entire country was to have elections to form a government, but only the South voted, and in the confused political climate, the South declared its independence of the North. The North, by this time under the military influence of the new Communist Chinese government, was quite happy to invade the South, and sent its troops to do battle there. Thus, the Korean War, which lasted till 1953, got off to a start.

From an ideological point of view, everything was clear cut from the beginning. It all had nothing to do with Korea. Korea was just a stage for the two actors, Russia (and China) on the one hand, and the US on the other. It was Communism versus Capitalism on display for the world to see. The US, frustrated by the Communist take-over of China, was determined to do its best to stop Communism spreading further in South East Asia. The Communists, encouraged by their military victory in China, were happy now to give up their former policy of infiltration and subversion in the region, and change over to an aggressive militaristic approach.

The early stages of the War, in July 1950, saw a gradual build-up in activities. The North made rapid progress and soon captured South's capital, Seoul, and proceeded further down the Korean peninsula. The Americans offered support to the South in the form of planes and warships. This quickly extended to the bombing of military sites in the North. In Australia, we too offered, and then provided, air and naval support, and at the same time announced that a number of youths would be called up for National Service some time in the future when suitable arrangements could be made for them.

Initially, both the US and Australia said no ground troops would be necessary. After a few weeks, the US changed its mind, and Australia followed a couple of weeks later. We knew things were getting serious when the papers starting showing little maps of military positions which had been all too familiar during WWII.

By the end of July, we had also committed another warship, and there was much interest in calling for volunteers to create a separate force for intervention.

Comment.   There seemed to be no interest among the so-called Great Powers in finding a diplomatic way out of the imbroglio. In fact, it looks like all parties were itching to get into it. For 33 years, Communism and Capitalism had been facing off. Right from the very first day of Communist rule in Russia, in 1917, the US had been opposed to the new regime, and had been involved with the White Army that tried to restore the Romanoffs to power.

Even in WWII, it was not certain for a while whether Russia would enter on the side of the Allies, and at the very end, in the Pacific War, it was the force of the atom bomb that blew the Russians off the fence. Now, it seemed that everyone was united in the delight of being free to fight at last. Not on their own territory, of course. But far from home, with no damage to their own civilians. The United Nations was clicking its tongue a bit, but was mainly involved at this stage with organising "observers" and, later, "peace-keepers".

So the War in Korea got off to a quiet start. Both sides thought it would soon be over, and that once they got really stuck into it, it would be a pushover. But, both sides were wrong, and two million deaths later, they stopped fighting and got back to where they started from. I will keep you informed periodically as the War gets into full swing.

The atom bomb now came into play. Various authorities and politicians in the US suggested that the best way to achieve peace was to drop a few bombs on North Korea, perhaps on military sites, or perhaps on major cities. Not everyone agreed that this should be done. Several Letters pointed out the barbaric nature of these suggestions, and how ineffectual they would be. But this Letter below raised a point, rarely heard up till now, that would become more prominent in future years.

Letters, Two Geneticists. We are surprised at the readiness with which apparently responsible people are advocating the use of the atomic bomb in the Korean dispute.

The public should be told of the undesirable effects that may result in a race subjected to atomic bomb attack. So far, no one has done so.

One of the most insidious effects of atomic radiation lies in the production of mutations or permanent changes in the hereditary factors which change our bodily characteristics. As is well known to most biologists, the great majority of these mutations are deleterious, and will remain temporarily hidden.

A large pool of these undesirable mutations, which must have been produced in the survivors of the atomic blast at Hiroshima, is at present hidden, but in time, with the spread of these undesirable factors throughout the population, they will begin to appear with horribly distressing results. If these terrible effects of atomic blast were generally known, no one with any sense of responsibility would advocate using the atomic bomb, for it would be a diabolical crime against future generations.

SEAMEN'S UNION BAD MISTAKE - DETAILS

At the start of the Korean War, the Seamen's Union in Australia was very firmly in the hands of Communists. The Executive of this Union met, and unanimously agreed that the Union should ban all shipments to aid the nation's involvement in Korea. This edict was to cover food, medical supplies and war materials.

The rank-and-file seamen immediately reacted against this decision. For example, on July 12, seven interstate ships in Sydney held meetings, and men on each of them voted unanimously to oppose the ban. This happened over two weeks, on all ships to use Australian ports in that period. One sailor captured the general mood. "We are all Australians. A lot of us fought in the last War, and we are not going to leave our men overseas without the things they need to stay alive. The Communists might like that, but they should stick to getting us better working conditions."

The Federal Secretary of the Union, Mr E Elliott, refused to accept the petition from grass-roots seamen's meetings, and the Federal Cabinet acted immediately. It decided to prosecute the Union's Executive, under the Crimes Act, which made provisions for imprisonment of up to four years for the sedition threatened here.

This was pressure that was too much to resist. The Executive gave in. They issued this defiant statement.

> The Seaman's Union condemns the dictatorial decision of Mr Menzies, ordering Australian naval seamen to submit to orders from the USA in its blatant armed interference in the domestic affairs of the Korean people. The US's declared objective is to wage aggressive war in all spheres, using the armed forces of other nations. In Korea, the Americans will fight to the last Australian.
>
> Australian seamen declare that they are opposed to Australia being plunged into this aggressive war, which can only mean disaster for our youth, and we urge other workers to join us in this opposition.

But, note that there was no mention of a ban on carrying materials to the Korean sphere. The Communists simply sidled out of the matter. After their heavy loss in the miners' strike the previous year, it was another embarrassing back-down for the Reds.

THE NEW SPORT: SPEAR FISHING

Letters. PISCES. For years now I, with many similarly minded people, have enjoyed "dropping in a line" at a comparatively sheltered bay near Sydney, and to date, apart from the capriciousness of the fish and the usual vagaries of the weather, nothing has occurred to mar this peaceful scene.

At the week-end, however, all of this was shattered by a begoggled party armed with guns of a type, and who I believe are politely termed **spear fishermen**.

These people were apparently possessed with insatiable appetites or hordes of friends and relatives, since, leaping from rock to rock with fantastic ability, they would plunge into the ocean ever so frequently, to emerge at intervals with their prey, and desisted only when so weighted down with fish there seemed to be a real danger of their incurring some physical strain.

Now this particular bay has been used for many years and would have continued to be used by anglers content to catch one or two fish. Many of these, too, are unable by reason of age or some disability to pursue any more active pastime, and it is on behalf of such people that I wish to voice a really serious protest.

Those in a position to know realise that the continued practice of spear fishing can only quickly result in areas, so misguidedly used, being completely denuded of fish. And the methods! Your sportsman does not, I am reliably informed, shoot a sitting duck. How much less, then, would he take one that swims within reach of his trigger finger. To-day, Izaak Walton must be stirring very uneasily where he lies.

Letters, F Cunliffe. A rather amusing jibe at spear fishermen in your pages implied that they were not sportsmen. Surely the definition of sportsman must include some reference to the element of personal risk relating to the sport concerned. My list of sportsmen would include all amateur athletes generally whose sport involves the element of personal danger. The list would **exclude** players of cards, chess, and snakes and ladders, all spectators of organised sport, punters and most line fishermen.

I must concede to PISCES that some line-fishing rock-hoppers do qualify as sportsmen, as they definitely incur risks at times. I know this well, having been a rock-hopper myself **before I introduced spear-gun fishing to this coast during 1937-38.**

The responsibility for depleting fish supplies lies with the black cormorants, who slay millions of tiddlers.

MIGRANTS GOING HOME.

Most migrants after the War had come out here on assisted passage, paying fares as low as ten Pounds, with a contract that might specify they **had** to stay three years. In early July, the Press carried reports that about ten per cent of European and British migrants were returning to their homes once their contract with the Australian Government expired. This came as something of a shock to the Australian population who generally assumed that every migrant would be delighted with all aspects of life in this utopia of ours. The writer below tells us why some migrants went home disappointed.

Letters, HAD IT. Your article, "Some Migrants coming for the Ride", did not mention the large number of migrants who have suffered financially and otherwise because of the failure of their **sponsors** to keep their part of the bargain.

I refer in particular to **the many relatives, friends, and others who guaranteed accommodation**, at any rate until the migrants found their footing and were able to look round for themselves. This accommodation often turned out to be a pig-sty or completely non-existent.

The alternative for many was to pay black market prices, which seem to flourish in Sydney, and hope that something else would turn up later. Far too often, nothing else does turn up, by which time a large sum has been extracted from slender savings. The immigration authorities express great concern over the plight of the less lucky migrants, but little seems to be done to assist them.

It should not be assumed that all returning migrants are awkward types, many are just disgusted with the apathetic attitude of many Australians and the primitive conditions existing outside the city proper.

SP BETTING

In 1950, Australia maintained a wonderfully efficient system of SP betting right across the nation every race-day. Gambling was legal on the track, but strictly forbidden anywhere else. Punters simply loved the thrill of gambling on horses on those days, and got an even greater thrill out of thwarting the flying squads, and other police raids on every pub and other SP venue they could find.

Letters, Hubert Allison. Glancing through one of this week's papers, I read with positive horror the suggestion of the chairman of the Sydney Turf Club, that Australia should hold regular mid-week racing fixtures.

I wish to protest most strongly against any such move.

With preposterous presumption, Mr Tancred glorifies this unadulterated gambling racket with the honourable title of "industry." What kind of industry is it that wrecks lives, homes, and careers with its inimitable lust for easy cash that blatantly and openly encourages people to flout the laws of the land.

I fear that Mr Allison's protest went unheeded in the long run, because there are something like fifty mid-week race meetings in Australia every week nowadays. But now, many years later of course, most of the SP betting has gone because the ubiquitous, but legal, TAB took over.

FIGHTING OUT OF A PAPER BAG

Boxing was a sport that drew very big audiences in 1950. Every State capital city had one night reserved for a major bout, and half a dozen preliminaries. Capacity crowds always turned up, and the events were broadcast via radio to an avid audience State-wide. Betting on the result was normal, and as blood rushed to various heads, a fight or two within the stadium crowd was expected.

The fighters themselves were always from the poorer ranks of society, and they saw boxing as being their way out of the poverty that their parents had endured. Everyone who stepped into a ring initially had a secret desire to become a champion, but after a few bouts knew well that in most cases the most he could hope for would be to earn a crust from the sport.

But there were champions, at the national level and at the international level. **World title** fights were always broadcast live, and the nation stopped while these battles went on. World Heavyweight Champions, liked Joe Louis, were remembered, "forever".

In short, apart from the corruption that is inevitable when people get together, it was all good clean healthy fun. But some people thought it might have a darker side.

Letters, Nina Lowe. I wish to thank you for printing Mr Ward's protest against professional boxing. We lift pious hands in horror at the very idea of bull-fighting, but flock in our thousands to see these debasing fights.

This bestial brutality with its every loathsome detail blazoned forth through the wireless, in a voice shaking with savage delight, enters our very homes.

Thousands of children listen to this sort of thing. "He's taking terrible punishment ... the crowd terribly excited ... listen to them ... He's just pouring blood ... all over his face and chest, too ... He ... he ... Yes, he's had it."

Our children at least should be protected from such horror.

There were quite a few apologists for the sport.

Letters, E King. Nina Lowe should turn the wireless off or to switch to another station.

As regards children being forced to listen to such dreadful broadcasts, I have heard portions of **the serials** that parents allow their children to listen to night after night, so that the broadcast of a boxing match would not do much harm; in any case children should be in bed at 9.15 p.m., when the boxing matches come on the air. I also wonder has the lady in question ever seen or read about our football (or should I say bootbrawl) matches of late.

Letters, Uppercut. It should be remembered that Homo Sapiens is by nature a fighting animal. A public stadium with a police sergeant and a medical officer at the ringside, and a competent referee inside the ropes with the boxers to see that the rules of fair-play are observed and undue punishment is not inflicted, provides a safety valve for this pent-up human instinct.

Admittedly accidents have occurred in the ring. But far more fatal accidents occur in the home than in the ring during the course of a year. **Is that any reason why we should ban homes?**

Australia may again have to fight for her national existence against a formidable foe from overseas, sooner perhaps than many imagine. Banning boxing and encouraging our youth to shrink and recoil with horror at the sight of trickle of "claret" is no way to train them for the task of defending their country.

Comment. Boxing, as with so many other activities, gradually fell out of mass popularity with the advent of TV. It also suffered as various other bodies came and went that said that **they** were the official bodies to issue world titles. Ordinary punters lost their interest in the world spectacles, and this affected local support.

AUGUST NEWS ITEMS

The NSW Marbles Association is planning to run the **first national tournament** soon. It has approached marbles bodies in other States, and expects that all of them will accept an invitation to attend. Contestants will be required to complete in a **nominated series of five events** that require a range of skills. They will **be free to use their own marbles**, but these must conform to published standards for each event.

Albert Namatjira came to Darwin for his first sight of the sea. He tasted it, pulled a face, and said "no good to drink." But, he added, "it is good to paint.".

Various Australian professors and also ICI Chemicals in Britain are talking about **artificial fibres taking over from wool**. They claim that research is showing that escaping gases from **the distillation of petrol** can be captured and made to produce materials with the same qualities as wool and silk. This is nasty talk for the wool trade here, and while **the end product will be a few years off, is causing much disquiet within the industry.**

The Cricket Test Match series against the Brits, scheduled for next year, **might not be broadcast** by either the *ABC* or the commercial radio stations. The **ball-by-ball description is very popular** and its removal would be a national disaster....

The problem is that the Cricket Board of Control wants a broadcaster who will pay fees for the privilege. The various stations are saying no way. In fact, I know that in the end **they did pay up,** and that set the trend for all sports in future, and for TV when it arrived....

Think of the millions of dollars paid now for the rights to broadcast sports.

The Food for Britain Fund has been closed. This **Fund was set up four years ago so that donors of money could give cash,** from which bundles of goods would be bought, and given to Brits to extend their food ration. **Over 8 million bundles were donated.** They typically included tinned goods, and jellies, jams, and honey. This was a different scheme from **Bundles for Britain.** In that case, **individuals here sent their own bundles direct to a family in Britain. But that was during the war....**

Both these schemes were greatly appreciated in Britain, and I add that even now **I get old-timer migrants telling me of how important the Bundles were in keeping morale high in wartime Britain.**

August 15th. It was announced that **Princess Elizabeth had given birth to a daughter.** Both were very well. Photos taken show Prince Phillip looking as pleased as he normally does on these occasions.

British newspapers were **suggesting that Princess Margaret will announce her engagement to the Earl of Dalkeith** in a few days. It might have already been announced, they say, but for the birth of the new Royal baby. **It turns out that the papers were wrong and indeed, they were wrong about half a dozen times, with similar forecasts, in the future.**

TERROR IN THE PLAZA

I was brought up in a small coal-mining town called Abermain. It was a happy little village of just over 2,000 people, and almost everyone got their money from the local coal pits. It was full of scarcely-educated but delightfully civilised Pommies, who had come here with their families and, 50 years later, still called Abermain their home. It was a closed town. There were no new arrivals, and no one left. The big towns near us were Cessnock, five miles to the West, and Maitland twenty miles East.

Abermain was not, as a rule, noted for its nightlife. It did have movies on Saturday afternoon and night, and a different program on Wednesday night. And of course, there was housie-housie on Thursday nights. But generally, all the men in town had to get up at five in the morning to get themselves off for another day of fresh air and sunshine down the pits. The women were nearly exhausted from worrying about whether the menfolk would be killed that day, and where the next quid would come from. So there was not much energy left over for high jinks in the evenings.

Saturday night, though, was different. For five years around 1950, Abermain became the Mecca for all the twinkle-toed Fred-and-Ginger aspirants in the coalfields. The hourly double-decker buses from Maitland and Cessnock brought in an 8 o'clock swell of people, young and old, all in their dancing pumps, ready to trip the light fantastic at the Old Time Dance in the Plaza Hall.

Now, this was an easy hall to trip in. It was about the size of two basketball courts, with a stage upfront, just like thousands of old halls round the nation. For the dance, however, the pine floor had been scrupulously cleaned and then sprinkled with candle grease and sawdust, ready for the great sliding competitions that preceded the dancing every week. If you ran, and then started to slide, you could go on for fifteen yards. If you ran and tripped, you broke your arm or some other part of your body. I chuckle nowadays when I hear TV people talking in awe about extreme sports as if they were new.

Then came the dancing. What a great programme there was for all to enjoy. It always started, of course, with "God Save the King." Then the MC came into play. "Take your partners, please, for an Old Time Waltz." After ten minutes of getting dizzy, spinning first to the left, and then reversing, dancers recovered for five minutes, and were ready for the intricacies of the Pride of Erin, the Canadian Three Step and the Boston Two Step, and the ultimate in slide-and-crash, the Gipsy Tap. On three occasions during the night, a "modern" dance was proclaimed, so that those a bit braver than the rest would have a go at the Quickstep, the Foxtrot, and the cuddly Jazz Waltz. For all of these, down in the two corners near the band, the really daring young folk would do remarkable stuff like jiving, and jitterbugging, and showed parts of their clothing and bodies that were scarcely fit for viewing at an Old time Dance.

The Barn Dance was the one that got everyone up to their feet. Two hundred people, all ages, and all three sexes, took up with partners and did a musical round of this wonderfully sophisticated dance. Two halted steps forward, two back, then two full twirls of waltz, then the two forward and two back again. Then came the real buzz of excitement. **The dance was made progressive, and that meant that**

after the final two forward, everyone changed partners. Whacko, you say. Here, over a period of an half hour, is the chance to dance with all the opposite numbers in the hall. What an opportunity.

There were, however, some drawbacks. For a young lad of 16 years like me, the married ladies with whalebone corsets were horrible to hold. I would rather have spun round with the whale. The hoity-toity attractive young ladies who curled their lips slightly when I came into view were not good for my tender ego. The strawberry blonde, aged about thirty, and well endowed, who came in real close and danced with a prominent pelvis, embarrassed me no end. My mother said she hated the men who stank of grog, and particularly tobacco. All in all, it was a wonderful event, done in every part of Australia at every dance in those days, and despite the fact that human bodies were in close contact, seemed to have made that generation no more lustful than any other.

The other big event was the First Set. Here four couples got themselves into a square, and pulverised each other for twenty minutes. Each man would short-arm swing his opposite lady until the lady's feet left the floor and hit some other dancer in the jaw or other tender spot. And in the last desperate effort to pick a winner, competitors would get into a small circle of eight, arms and bodies enmeshed, and rotate at a fast speed until the atom was finally smashed and all four couples fell to the ground panting. More body contact; but no one seemed to mind in those days.

Now that you know what the Plaza was, what about **the terror** I mentioned? Well, the terror I am talking about is my personal terror, a terror that burst upon me at every

Plaza dance I went to. **Firstly,** it hit me when I had to ask some lovely-looking girl for a dance. Of course, most of the time, there was no problem fronting Mum, or some of the married ladies who more or less taught me to dance. Nor, indeed, with some of the younger girls that I knew well. But when someone popped up who was new and pretty, or was not so new but way above me, then terror of public rejection became almost crippling. Will I go right across the floor and ask this goddess to jump into my arms? If she says no, surely every person in town will be watching. Then I will have to walk back to my seat again, humiliated. What if she sneers and turns to her girl-friend, and completely ignores me, or simply laughs? This was common enough. Is she worth the risk? Yes, yes, she is worth it. Here goes.

I must say that I got quite a few knock-backs, and they hurt. But, I must also say that none of them were as offensive as I feared. So, maybe my terror alert was a false alarm, but I can tell you it did not seem like it at the time.

Terror came again when they announced a Ladies' Choice. This was one or two dances a night when the ladies had to get out of their bunker and cross the floor and ask a male for a dance. My problem was that I was a tall skinny kid, and had no secret admirer. Very quickly, all the good-looking young blokes were up dancing, and the number of young girls still on the prowl was quickly diminishing. Would someone, please, come and get me? Would I be left sitting here, alone, the only youth who could not get a partner? For many a night I would have been, except for a couple of the married women who were kind and wise enough to come to the rescue. At that stage, the whalebones were really welcome.

Meanwhile, unaware of the drama unfolding, the four-piece band played on. Young Harry, the leader, played the trumpet and cornet, and crooned. He was notorious for singing a little, absolutely meaningless, ditty that went:

> All the cowhands want to marry Harriet,
> Harriet's handy with a larriot,
> But she don't want to marry yet,
> She's having too much fun. ……

Young Harry was a good-looking 35-year old, and had a nice manner and winning smile. I suppose that explains why he always got claps and cheers when he sang this, and why there were always calls for him to do it again. He obliged every time.

Old Harry, his father, was the drummer. He had a big base drum, with the foot pedal, and four kettle drums, and little triangles that he tinkled at times. He was unusual for a drummer, because he had only one arm, and always said that he was lucky because if he had two, he would need **eight** kettle drums. I am still not sure if I follow his logic.

Halt-time served two purposes. It allowed **everyone a chance to refresh** and get their energy back. So 200 people charged down to Lofthouse's Café, with one shilling and threepence in their kitty, and feasted on such luxuries as ice cream sodas, and banana splits. A few stocked up on Craven A or Camel cigarettes, and even fewer got some roll-your-own Log Cabin tobacco. **The second activity at half-time** was to open up the hall and get rid of the cigarette smoke that had gradually built up over the last two hours. By now it was at the point where pit canaries would have turned up their toes. The floor was also swept thoroughly, and the accumulated cigarette butts, a mountain of them, were taken away. I never saw a woman or girl smoking at a Plaza dance.

At midnight, the double-deckers took the travellers back to Cessnock and Maitland. The band and a few others went into the back room and drank too much beer, and my Dad swept the hall again, and also drank too much beer. It was all over, and ready for next week.

Let me add a few post-scripts. Firstly, there was terror among the young women too. Many have told me of how dreadful it was to be sitting on their bench, and to look up and see a young buck, whom they hated or feared, staring fixedly at them, and making a bee-line for them. Where do I hide? What do I say: Go away, I hate you? You stink of grog? I want to dance with Albert Hindmarsh; I'm sure he'll ask me if only you will go away? Finally, would he get nasty if I say no? This was always on the cards. Rarely, but still a possibility.

Secondly, for five years Abermain Plaza was **the** place to dance on a Saturday night. After that, the Catholic priest at Cessnock was persuaded that this type of dancing was not quite so sinful and so he opened up the Catholic Hall, in a much bigger town, to the same people who ran the Abermain dance. So, that was the end of that for Abermain.

Thirdly, for those of you concerned about my welfare, I am happy to say that as I grew, I put on some weight, and gradually grew to a size where Fuzzy from Port Moresby would have got a decent meal out of me. My popularity among the girls grew proportionately with my weight, and in retrospect, I wonder why I did not seek to get as fat as a pig. In any case, I moved up to about average in the popularity stakes, and so ended that particular reign of terror.

Fourthly, Saturday night at the Plaza was replicated at a thousand venues right across the nation. Whole families trotted out together and went to the same place. Somehow even the boys learned to dance, and some of the important lessons of civilised behaviour were ingrained by example. It seems to me a great pity that such nights are hard to find nowadays. Apart from the young people doing their mating rituals at pubs and the like, we now seem to spend Saturday night watching TV. I suppose there is nothing the matter with that, but for my part, I miss the wonderful fun of all the great community events we used to have.

GREAT ADVICE FROM THE USA

The Korean situation stirred up more talk in the US about **atom bombs**. The US Atomic Energy Commission, trying to allay fears of the Bombs, issued a small **456-page manual** that described things that happened during explosions. It offered the reader the advice that "an increased illumination tells you that a bomb has gone off." It mentioned that "loose, white clothing gives good protection," so, I presume, if you have time to change, then tennis clothes would be quite acceptable. During the actual attack, "hit the dirt immediately, do not look at the light flash, roll into a ball for protection, stay put for ten seconds, and if you can avoid fatal injury for another minute, you have survived."

About radiation it said "Persons exposed to radiation should refrain from begetting offspring for two to three months after the explosion, to **reduce** the probability of transmitting aberrations in chromosomes to the next generation." Good advice, I believe, but most experts today think that the delay should be measured in years or lifetimes.

The American Press reported that the booklet failed to allay the alarm over the deadly bombs, and in fact did quite the opposite by making more people aware of their effects.

NUTRITION IS IN THE NEWS

The latest on diets. Nutrition was getting into the news more and more as our standard of living allowed us the luxury of finding new matters to worry about. You will quickly realise that information on the perfect diet was just as confused and silly then as it is now.

Letters, Portia Geach, Progressive Housewives Association. Now that the price of food is so high, may I suggest to the worried housewife the great value of economical wheatmeal, which will build good teeth and bone and keep the family well fed.

A large plate of well-cooked porridge, plus milk and honey, will send the children off to school well fed and happy. For the very young, strain the porridge.

Wheatmeal or wholemeal bread with fillings of raisins, dates, or simple centres, and with **the glass of milk that the Government provides**, will take care of the mid-day meal, and at night a simple meal will round off the day well.

Try it, and see how the children thrive and keep good tempered.

Letters, George Dupain. Miss Geach should know that the effect of such a diet is to lower the nutritional status of people, not raise it.

Cereals contain a substance (phytin) which interferes with the absorption of calcium in the diet. A diet excessive in cereals is likely to affect bone and tooth development.

Indeed, warnings have frequently been uttered by nutritionists that the human race has reached the limits of safety in its ingestion of cereals. **Man is not a bird, and he cannot live on seeds.** He is an omnivore, with carnivorous leanings.

The only compensation for the use of cereal is to add an excess of calcium to the diet, either in the form of milk, milk powder, or some calcium compound.

WOOL PRICE RISE

Wool prices rose about fifty per cent at the start of the wool-selling season in Sydney, compared to their price at this time last year. Buyers and brokers described it as "the most amazing sale ever."

Wool that was bringing 66 pence a Pound last year, and 114 pence a Pound in June, sold today for 168 pence a Pound. US buyers were not active, and it could be that further major increases will be expected if they do return to the market. Experts warned that, while this increase was good for the nation, and for the farmers, it was certain to increase inflation, and that various authorities must become aware of that.

Comment. This was the beginning of a few years of boom in wool prices. The US **did** come into the market, and prices **did** increase further. The reason was that Korea became bitterly cold in Winter, and all of the soldiers, on both sides, had to be kept warm in wonderful wool. **Australia was in for a great ride on the sheep's back.**

Wet blanket on wool. At the same time as this wool boom entered its infancy, Professor Heater, of the School of Chemical Engineering at Sydney University, was getting headlines by warning that synthetics were being developed that would replace wool. The new products would come from petroleum, and be an extension of the processes used to create nylon. He pointed out that no woman in Sydney would dream of wearing silk stockings if she could get nylon. The same will happen with artificial wool.

Comment. Professor Heater was canvassing for more money for research for his own department, while at the same time telling the truth. His prophesy did become substantially correct, with synthetics now having a very large share of the market. But they did not replace wool completely, and wool too has a reasonable market share, especially in high fashion.

PLAYING IN THE STREETS

In the 1940's, it was common for lots of Aussies to play cricket, footie, hopscotch, handball, marbles, tennis, rounders, and Red Rover in the street.

By 1950, there were too many cars to do this. And thus, many adults started to become safety conscious.

In any case, the number of player started to drop off. And then, in 1956, TV put an end to it all.

NEWS AND VIEWS

Australia wins back the Davis Cup. We had lost the Cup to the Americans in 1946. Since then, our attempts to get it back had been valiant, but futile, with players like John

Bromwich and Billy Sidwell doing their best. This year, we included the handsome youngsters, Frank Sedgeman and Ken McGregor, in the Team, and it brought home the bacon. Australia won the tie by four rubbers to one, and started us on a Golden Age of tennis.

Birth of Princess Anne. August 15th. Large crowds gathered outside Buckingham Palace and Clarence House in London to welcome news of the birth of a new Princess. But the fact that it was headline news in Australia shows how great the interest was here too. The Royal Family was very popular in Australia.

Comment. Anne remained in relative obscurity. She is about 15th in line for the throne.

Letters, PRESBYTERIAN. I turned on my radio yesterday morning to a commercial station and heard a record of a song entitled, "Will There Be Any Yodeling in Heaven?" It was sung by some females who called themselves The Girls of the Golden West.

In the song, the Almighty was referred to as the Great Ranger, and it was suggested that the saints greet new arrivals in Heaven with hideous yodeling sounds.

Could bad taste go any further than this blasphemous performance?

Food for Britain to cease. The Chairman of the Fund to send bundles of food to Britain has said that the Fund will probably close in the New Year, when current stocks of food have been used up. Ernie O'Dea said the Fund had sent 3 million parcels in the last three years, but now that Britain was receiving an increased food supply, there was less need for it.

Comment.   Since 1945, Australians had donated bundles of food for Britain in a quite unselfish manner. Despite difficulties caused by postal authorities in Australia and Britain in the early years, they had persisted in sending these food parcels in huge numbers. The fact that O'Dea said that he was still sending 40,000 per month, just from Sydney, indicates how generous the public had been.

Keep the punters off my tram.   Letters, J Hart.
When race meetings are held at Randwick on week days, many thousands of human drones are disgorged upon the already overloaded transport system of Sydney at a time when workers are homeward bound.

These same workers are being, almost daily, exhorted to step up production as the country's greatest need. It seems monstrous that they have to stand and watch buses and trams laden with race-goers go past while they wait for transport to take them home after a day's work.

If Mr McGirr feels permits mid-week racing, then it behoves him to take steps to see that racing clubs arrange their fixtures to finish not later than 3pm.

SEPTEMBER NEWS ITEMS

Truck drivers in NSW are unhappy. Traffic regulations were issued years ago, and have not kept up with modern times. For example, t**rucks with a load over 11 tons may not travel over 15 miles per hour.** Police still enforce this rule when it suits them....

Twenty-five 25 heavy lorries, loaded with blue metal to exceed the load limit, took off in convoy and drove at **15 miles per hour from Penrith to Parramatta**. This was a distance of 20 miles. Hundreds of vehicles backed up behind them. Motorists and police were not impressed....

Many truck drivers were booked by police. A traffic sergeant said "they will not only be booked. **They will be locked up.**"

Demand for lottery tickets had doubled in the last five years. In NSW, a drawing will now be held on Saturdays for the first time. Officials say the extra demand shows that people are feeling much more prosperous, and are losing **their fear of depressions and recessions from the pre-war era.**

A young Dutch migrant girl, on her way to Australia, **brought a white cocky with her**. In Indonesia, it received a clean Bill of Health from authorities, but **on arrival in Darwin it was strangled**. The health inspector was very nice, but explained that Australian regulations forbade its entry....

Darwin residents are indignant because thousand s of these cockies fly in from Indonesia every day in season.

Normally they do not carry **Bills of Health with them.**
September 7th. Legacy's War Orphans Appeal is set
to start with a great deal of fan-fare. For example, in
Sydney, **5,000 volunteers** will **sell badges in the streets**
tomorrow, and 39 girls from the Bank of NSW will be
given the day off to help. One Sydney businessman has
donated one thousand Pounds. He has done so every
year for the eight years of the Fund....

Legacy **in NSW alone** helps to support **4,700 families,
including 9,300 children, whose fathers gave their
lives in war.**

Radio personality, **Bob Dyer, will star in a new show
from March next year**. It will be sponsored by Colgate
Palmolive, and he will be **paid 33,000 Pounds a year.**
This will be **a record** for a radio star in Australia. **Hi -
Ho Everybody, its off to bank we go.**

The Pastures Protection Board said that **a saucer of beer**
left out overnight will keep your gardens **safe from a
new variety of slugs**.

September 24th, **News from Korea.** As the inevitable
confusion in the war zone in Korea went on, **US planes
bombed and strafed British troops**. 160 Brits were
killed or wounded.

Children under the age of 10 have never tasted rice.
This is because of war needs for Britain and for our Asian
allies, like India. Now our Government says it may be
sold here once again. Shops should have it in stock
within a week, and it should remain available thereafter.

THE WOOL LEVY

News item, Canberra,   Professor Douglas Copeland, Vice Chancellor of the Australian National University, said today that a tax of 33 per cent should be imposed on wool growers to help problems created by the current high prices for wool. He said that with such high prices, all woolgrowers could afford such an impost, and it was absolutely necessary to avoid the inflation that would follow when all the wool cheques were received in the nation.

Obviously, wool-growers did not think highly of this garbled proposal, and they said so through the Letters columns of the papers.

Letters, H Davis. I can't make head or tail out of all the proposals that have come from Copeland's suggestion for ripping off wool-growers. He says he wanted to take 33 per cent, and that while most of it would go to tax, a bit might be held and repaid a few years later when things get tough again. Other people say that maybe some of it would be taken away and given to someone else, who would do clever things like marketing and research with it.

I don't like any of these. I grew my wool this year, just like the last 23 years, in the hope of making enough money to pay off some of my debt. Now, everyone wants to change the rules. Everyone wants my money.

When I get my cheque, do you know what I'll do with it? I'll pay off some of my debt to the bank. And if I get another good cheque next year, I'll pay off some more. Then in the years after my debt has gone, I'll get some decent fences, and after that, maybe some fertiliser. It will be 23 years before I can add anything to inflation by wild spending.

Have a look at it, mate. There are 71,000 wool-growers who have 30 bales or less. And of these 71,000, there are 72,000 with a bank debt you can't jump over. Copeland and his mob would be better suggesting extra taxes for the stock market. After all, that adds nothing of value. Does wool? Too right it does and you know it.

Letters, Campbell Garrett. During the years of depressed wool prices, when wool was averaging 6 pence a pound, there was never any suggestion by politician, economist, or general public that the grower of wool should be subsidised.

But now, we have the spectacle of astute politicians and theoretical economists devising weird and wonderful ways of depriving the woolgrower of what one would almost describe, judging by these grand gentlemen's utterances, as his "ill-gotten gains", and forcing him to subsidise the use of wool.

If it is the question of excess profit, why should the politician stop at the wool-growing industry? Why not pursue their activities into, say, the motor distribution industry, which has been for many years enjoying an unprecedented boom?

With all the political propaganda among politicians and others, and all the wailing and gnashing of teeth among the general public, there is another side to consider. What about the flow of a large volume of money into the country. By not interfering with the wool-grower, it will be found that the large portion of his surplus income will be expertly used for improving his property. This will increase production and in turn make a favourable contribution to checking inflation.

The final aspect is the proposed imposition of a super-tax on any one section of the community could conceivably create a most undesirable precedent and could easily react to the detriment of other sectors of the community and, in the future, create an uncomfortable position for them.

Letters, W McCurrie. This might be the golden opportunity for a back-to-land year for our young people.

As I have travelled on business throughout most of this State, I have been struck by the monotonous state of the disrepair of most boundary fences. The grazier has had to live on his capital more or less since Customs duties were introduced in early Federation days, and it has been quite impossible for him to keep his improvements up to the standard of 50 years ago.

A man can only do manual work for a given number of years. After that, he must pay for it to be done, and the ranks of young men who can do this work are very depleted. This year of prosperity may well be the answer to decentralisation.

Comment. Arthur Fadden was Treasurer and also leader of the Country Party. He was supposed to be protecting the interests of graziers, but **he seemed more worried about collecting revenue**. He came up with a taxation formula that did take a great deal, maybe about 30 percent of net revenue, from farmers, and another 15 per cent for research and promotion. Sadly for him, he could not start this scheme immediately because, guess what, the Labor Party blocked it in the Senate. But in the next year or so he did succeed, and **this was the beginning of the wool levy, and it still continues today.**

Granted, farmers get some money back in the poorer years, and it is good to that extent. But to me it seems that **before the scheme was put into operation,** Fadden would have been advised to gracefully let the farmers have a few years without any super-taxes to fix the problems mentioned in the Letters above. But his haste to introduce it was obvious to all. There can be no doubt that the gradual demise of the Country Party dated from this time, as some voters with long memories vowed that they would never vote for that Party again.

NO NEW WORLD WAR

News item, London, Sept 13.   Britain's Prime Minister, Clement Attlee, said today that he expected that a **third** World War could be avoided. "Many people here in Britain, and others overseas, claim that a new conflagration is inevitable. I think they are wrong. It is true that the Communist menace is potentially a threat to world peace, and the current hostilities in Korea, if they get out of hand, could lead to serious consequences. But if we all keep a level head, and persist in our current determination that peaceful means be found, we can avoid war."

Comment. Attlee was really responding to another suggestion, this time by a military person in the US Administration, that a large city in Korea should be bombed, "like Hiroshima to teach the Koreans a lesson once and for all." Fortunately, people on both sides of the Atlantic did keep a level head, and in fact, in this case, the official who suggested the bombing "was spoken to by the President."

URANIUM FOUND IN AUSTRALIA

Every country in the world with a big hammer was by now trying to split the atom, and many of them realised that they had a better chance if the atom was a uranium atom. So, demand for uranium increased enormously. We quickly recognised that we had the geographic formations that could be suitable for producing the ore, and our fossickers went off to wild parts to have a look. In quick succession, they found commercial deposits in the Northern Territory at Rum Jungle, and at the Ferguson River. The quality of the ore was very good, and the deposits were extensive. Washington and London quickly signalled that they were interested in the finds, and high level talks with them were scheduled in the near future.

The Menzies Government was quite excited by this. It was keen on joining the small band of nations, centred on America, who formed the Atom Bomb Club. The US had made it clear **that Australia could not join**, and said it was because of the fear that our **security** was not good enough, so that secrets of bomb-production would find their way to the Russians. **Now**, Menzies hoped that if we could supply the Western World with high grade uranium, then he could bargain his way into the Club. As it turned out, despite his efforts over 20 years, Australia never did gain entry, and we remain, for better or worse, outside.

RICE BACK ON THE MENU

During the War, many commodities were rationed. **Rice was not one of them.** Instead, rice consumption was forbidden for the entire nation, and whatever rice we produced was shipped off to Brits, who presumably liked their rice puddings more than we did. The only exception was that if persons were able to get medical prescriptions saying that rice was essential to their health, then they could get a moderate amount that might last them a few weeks. Needless to say, the rigmarole of actually getting their hands on any of the verboten product was fraught with difficulties and arguments and frustrations.

Some of this can be seen in the following Letters. But note too, that here we were five years after the end of the War, and that the rice-denial system was still firmly in place. **Ending a War is kid's stuff compared to getting rid of war-time austerity.**

Letters, George Goodman. At the beginning of rice rationing, I have been told now, the allowance was 5 pounds for a period of three months, and then only if authorised on a doctor's certificate. It works out at just under an ounce per day. That is, two spoonfuls.

Last September, being affected by a stomach complaint, I was ordered rice, and received a parcel of 10 pound, but no advice as to how long it was supposed to last. I think I consumed about two ounces per day. As it was nearly finished, my doctor gave me a fresh certificate for one pound of rice for thirteen weeks. This was forwarded through the grocer to the rationing authority who replied that I should have to do without rice until the first week in April.

Under the Chifley Government, a clerk in a city office could override the certificate of a medical man. It looks like it will continue in the same way under a Menzies Government. Remember, it was little pin-pricks like this that swayed the adverse vote against Labor.

Letters, Medicus. The continued withholding of rice becomes more and more irritating, and is yet another example of the politician's determination to perpetuate the "shove around" of the public.

Rice can be considered to be an article of staple diet here, nearly as much as the coloured people up north, who benefit at our expense. They have had time enough, and more, to grow their own. Anyone going to New Guinea can see the natives **prodigating** their over-supply. They could grow their own, but know a good thing when they see it.

It is an infliction upon the poor, weary "string-bag brigade" that they should be denied rice, and it is fair to assume that, if available, rice would be in every kitchen cupboard in the Commonwealth, and what a stand-by for the housewife, both as regards cheapness and supply, if she could have at hand this type of dish of such multiple usages, as vegetable and sweet.

Charity should now clearly recommence at home. Rice should be a right, not a concession.

Letters, A S. During the last few days I have read in your columns quite a number of letters about rice. However, the public seems to be unaware of the fact that Australia could, at any time, since January 1st, import rice without any foreign currency implications.

But our Department of Trade does not issue import licences for this project. They do so for Russian caviar, Russian salmon and crabmeat, French asparagus and mushrooms, English jams and biscuits, but no licence for the importation of rice which is superior to the Australian rice anyway.

Letters, GP. I cannot say that your correspondent, who moans about rice, moves me to tears. Rice is not necessary for any stomach complaint, and no doctor has any business to give a certificate alleging that rice is necessary. I like rice, and many of my patients miss it, but they do not all come whingeing to me to give them a certificate to get something that is denied to others.

EISTEDDFODS AS ESCAPE ROUTES

Eisteddfods were annual events in all communities. In Sydney, 2,000 people, the majority of them children, competed for silver-plated cups that said they were the best in their age-group in singing, or tap dancing, or elocution, or playing the violin, or similar events. The whole event was grass-roots stuff, with entrants generally getting private training and encouragement, and spending hours and hours practising in their own homes.

In some country areas, the eisteddfod movement was very strong. Parents who were locked into certain poor areas were worried that their children might also become locked in. They were always casting round for some way of getting their children out of the poverty and dead-end jobs that they themselves were forced to put up with. The hope of many of these parents was that their children might just become good at something, and develop enough skill to make a break. It was a slight hope, but there were enough role-models who had done it to keep that dream alive.

TROUBLES IN MIGRANT CAMPS

Troubles in migrant camps. In 1950, the number of migrants coming from Europe had reached a peak. They were generally classified as being skilled workers, and most of them came out with financial assistance from the Australian Government. They were also given help with housing, and most of them ended up for a year or two in old army camps, in barracks, that had been converted to accommodate families. There these migrants were crowded, and living in conditions that were a lot worse than they had been used to before the War. Troubles were always brewing, and I enclose this report, not so much because it was typical, but just to remind you that their primitive conditions evoked primitive behaviour.

The Newcastle Court of Petty Sessions heard today that one Andre Milkovic had assaulted Jon Vanchkoff at Greta camp last night. Detective Woodford of Maitland told Judge O'Sullivan that Vanchkoff had been hit severely with a baton of wood about the head.

Mr Milkovic had been sent from the camp to perform a job in Queensland. The Detective indicated that this often happened at the Greta camp, and that it was the cause of considerable friction, because they left their wives behind for several months. In the conditions of the camp, with overcrowding, and little else to do, certain undesirable situations were constantly occurring.

Mr Milkovic had returned to camp, and had at first been unable to find his wife. Late in the evening, he saw her leaving a hut with Vanchkoff, and had then molested him and hit him with the baton. However, the woman was not in fact his wife, and Vanchkoff had called the police. The aggressor was placed on a good behaviour bond, and the Judge expressed regret that all too often, in migrant camps, the law was being taken into the hands of persons who did not have the wisdom they should.

NEWS AND VIEWS

Industrial disputes, Newcastle. Mr Hamilton Knight, Federal Conciliation Commissioner, heard yesterday that two disputes were holding up steamers in Newcastle.

The first involved the *River London*, where the Australian Shipping Board had refused requests for carpets in cabins, a different brand of bath soap, and stainless steel washbasins.

The demands also included ash trays in mess rooms, rubber instead of wooden bath mats, and tea issued in commercial packets instead of from bulk. Mr Knight said that nothing in the list of demands was worth tying a ship up for, and it was the most frivolous dispute he had seen.

On the second ship, the *S.S Lowana,* the men refused to sail unless the chief cook was replaced. No specific details of the chef's alleged shortcomings were available for the court, but he considered the attitude of the men unreasonable and untenable.

Comment. Industry was plagued with many such disputes, where pig-headedness was paramount on both sides. Here, knowing nothing more than the above about this dispute, it seems that some reasonable solution could be found at a trivial cost. Perhaps that was the job of the learned Commissioner, but unfortunately these gentlemen sometimes turned out to be agents for the bosses. In any case, such disputes were altogether too common, and festered and multiplied and spread. They were costing the nation a great deal.

The birth of the Sara Quads. Bellingen, Sept 17th.

Mrs Betty Sara gave birth to the first of four babies she is expecting in the next few days. The baby is about 12 days premature, and is in good condition. There is a wide expectation that the second child will be born in the next 24 hours, and that the third and fourth will arrive within hours of that. Her husband is an ambulance attendant at the local hospital, and an ex-POW from the European scene of the War.

Comment. These quads were conceived without any artificial additives. They were well marketed, and were given much-needed financial support by magazines and by sponsorship agreements. Photos of the quads were difficult to obtain because the Australian Womens' Weekly acquired rights to them prior to the births.

OCTOBER NEWS ITEMS

Well-regarded businessman and philanthropist, Sir Edward Hallstrom, was seeking exhibits for Sydney's Taronga Zoo. As Chairman of the Zoo, he **offered 75 Pounds to any fisherman who would sell him a largish shark**. It would then go on display. **A condition of sale was that the shark had to survive for a week....**

Two sharks, each about nine feet, had been offered, but **both died within a week, supposedly of shock**. **Hallstrom has withdrawn his offer** as a consequence. It appears that he did so because of economic considerations. There was **scarcely any sympathy for sharks within the community at this time.**

Johnny Weissmuller's face was badly cut in a car crash in California. **Every one knows all about Johnny,** so there is no need to tell you who he is. All I will say is that **he was a big man in my childhood days**, and I know that a man of his stature will recover quickly.

Our Federal politicians had been seeing **signs of inflation**. Prompted by the huge increases in the nation's wool cheque, and prices rising all over the place, they stewed for a month, talked a lot, held conferences, and finally came up with measures to slow inflation....

It turned out that they were a bit of a fizzer. They restricted themselves to raising taxes on luxury goods such as cars and jewellery. And the tax rate only went from 25 to 33 per cent on these. As the newspapers said "how can these such trivial moves **halt a problem that was supposed to be so big?**"....

One thing that came out of debates on this was it was became obvious that sales taxes on **wedding and engagement rings** were regarded as luxury items. **Do you agree that this should be so?**

The number of Tuberculosis (TB) cases reported is on the rise. Recent surveys have shown that if the number continues to increase, facilities in all States will not be adequate. Already, **sanatoria are filled with long waiting lists....**

Comment. The sad situation outlined above proved to be true. Over the next decade, the situation became critical, and was ultimately relieved only by the application of **BCG injections**....

Another comment. The same was true **for polio over the same period**. This time the saviour was the invention of the **Salk vaccine**.

Nine men were working on the face of the Burrinjuck Dam. **The ropes to their platform got twisted,** and it tilted. **The men were thrown off**, and fell into the flood-swollen Murrumbidgee River, 200 feet below. All of them were killed.

Early in this book, I said strikes were a constant pain in the neck. Well, I can tell you that they **still** were. **For example**, trains in **Melbourne** will stop all day on Friday. **South Australia and NSW** will stop out of sympathy on Monday. **There is no shortage of reasons given for the strikes. But no one cares about the reason. It is the strikes themselves that they dread and hate.**

KOREA AND THE RED BILL

Over the course of a month, events in Korea moved quickly. Australian troops **had been stationed in Japan** for three years as part of a peace-keeping force and, by chance, had been scheduled to be repatriated about now. Instead, they were sent from the relative delights of Tokyo to the fighting fields in Korea. **The Army propaganda machine** put a lot of effort into convincing people at home that the troops were ecstatic at this and that they were just bursting for the opportunity to get into battle. Real gung-ho, "Boys' Champion" stuff. But whether they liked it or not, and most of them did not, they arrived in Korea about the start of October.

There the situation had changed. The Americans had been previously herded into a corner on the south-east coast of the country. But by now, they had landed forces half-way up the peninsula and cut the north Korean forces off from **their** home state. So, by the time the Australians landed, the North Koreans were in full retreat, and in fact the South Koreans had just crossed the border and were chasing them towards their northern capital in Pyongyang.

The Americans were a bit coy for a few days about crossing the 38th parallel into the North. China and Russia had not, so far, sent any troops into battle, but might be provoked into doing so if they thought the Americans were set for the take-over of Communist territory. But the South Koreans kept charging into the North, and the big Reds made no protest, so the US decided to press ahead. All along the rapidly-advancing front, they met little opposition, and were soon to be heard bragging that the war was over, and it was now just a case of mopping up.

By the end of the month, they were at the border of Manchuria to the North, and bombing bridges that spanned rivers into China. They were very careful not to let the bombs stray across the border, of course, because that might stir the sleeping Chinese giant. But, the land battles went on, right up to the border one day, and then a withdrawal down South the next day, and then back again the following one.

During all this make-believe world of real slaughter, things were happening. China was slowly advancing on the border of Tibet. And it was doing the same thing on the border of Indo China. Both of these events meant trouble in the future. At the same time, China and Russia were massing troops inside China, ready to plunge into Korea. Anyone who thought the War there was almost over had another think coming.

Then, sadly, tragically, in Australia we started to get the little print-boxes in our daily papers that detailed the deaths and injuries to our own troops in Korea. Everyone had been familiar with these terrible messages every day of WWII, and had hoped never to see them again. But here they were once more, spreading terror and misery daily to those who had fighters in Korea. It was such a shock to see them there, and made every thinking person realise with horror that we were once again in a fair-dinkum war.

HIGH JINKS IN PARLIAMENT

By early October, Menzies had had a very nice time in London, Washington and Tokyo, and was ready to face Parliament again. **Three months had elapsed** since the

Labor-controlled Senate had rejected his anti-Red Bill, and so he was ready to introduce it again, and perfectly happy to have a double dissolution if it did not pass both Houses. So, he immediately brought it before the House of Representatives, where he had a big majority, and of course it flew through there.

Then he took it to the Senate. This was very unkind of him, because it caused the Labor Party no end of trouble. Half of their elected representatives wanted to pass it, and half did not. Likewise, three of the States wanted it passed unchanged, and the rest opposed it. Some wanted the Caucus of representatives to make the decision, some wanted the Senators only to make the decision, some wanted only the Shadow Cabinet to make it, and some wanted the whole national body of the Labor movement to vote on it. They got themselves into the type of mess that only the Labor Party can manage, and in the meantime, used their majority in the Senate to stall having a vote taken.

 But after two weeks, the inevitable day came, and the vote was taken, and the Bill passed. So the threat of a double dissolution had gone away. Or had it? After all, there were several other Bills floating round that the two Parties disagreed on. Surely Menzies could knock one of them into a shape that the Labor Party would have to reject.

And now, at least, the Liberals would be able to prosecute under the new anti-Red Act. Or would they? Certainly they could prosecute and get the desired results, but would the judgements stick? Was it not likely that the validity of the legislation would be challenged in the High Court and maybe found illegal? There were many, many Trade

Unions and their officials who would attract the attention of the Act. Surely someone would mount a serious legal challenge. And then perhaps it would succeed.

By the end of October, all of these uncertainties were swirling round, and all sitting Members were being very nice and helpful to the electors. In the meantime, these electors were watching with great interest all the unusually frantic goings-on, and many voiced their opinions through the Letters columns.

The first two Letters were not at all concerned about such matters as the Red-bill nor about a possible double dissolution. The first one was upset about all the political radio broadcasts that would threaten his evening listening. The second writer said he didn't like the first.

Letters, Not Listening.   Without a by-your-leave, every station, commercial and National, may be taken over at a moment's notice by Members of Parliament and our evening spoilt.

There is one very important factor that seems to be overlooked by those who take for granted that we listen. We do not have to. However much we may be interested in the statements of the Prime Minister or any Minister, we like to choose the time or place to hear them. The evening, when one is tired and perhaps preferring some relaxation, may not be the time.

Letters, P Stevenson. I fear for the well-being of our country when such wretched stupidity as that displayed by **Not Listening** perpetuated.

Surely, it is the duty of every citizen who has this country's welfare at heart to listen when the Prime Minister speaks to the nation on matters of gravest importance to us all.

For the petty mindedness of such as NOT LISTENING, I have nothing but contempt, but I also fear his kind, for such shallow thinking will not help to pull us through the tremendous national problems now facing us.

Other Letter writers addressed more serious issues.

Letters, H Fell.   Not only is a double dissolution of the Parliament   imperative, but the people should be given an opportunity of expressing their views **on the abolition of the Senate itself**. I would urge the Government to introduce a Bill immediately for the taking of a referendum on this issue. It could hardly be opposed by Labor, as it is part of their policy.

It is not merely the Menzies Government that is being thwarted by the Senate majority. It is the people themselves, who less than a year ago expressed their desires quite clearly at the poll. The same voters will soon end this farce if given a chance.

Letters, N Edwards. One important function of the Senate is to represent the people who voted in the previous election. We always say that the new Parliament should represent the views of the voters at the time of the elections, but we should also provide for the consideration of voters who are of the past. The six-year overlapping term of office provides for this. In other words, just because a Party wins in the House, it should not mean that they can throw out everything that came before them. Having a rump in the Senate, stops this.

To say that the Senate must be just a replica of the House is surely ignoring a very important part of our system of checks and balances.

Comment. The idea of a double dissolution continued to fester. The idea of the dissolution of the Senate faded out.

THE MERRY-GO-ROUND

This was a period of increased economic activity and prosperity. The Korean War meant that wool and wheat were fetching record prices and other commodities were doing much the same thing. Capital was flowing into the nation, there were jobs for everyone, and something of a housing boom was on the cards. Even the Basic Wage had been increased by a whole Pound a week just now.

But someone always spoils the party. We have already seen how the Federal Government was gearing up to dun the sheep farmers. On top of that, the State Governments were all putting up fares, the Commonwealth was raising taxes on "luxury" goods, and inflation was taking with one hand most of the benefits gained on the other.

So, the Letter writers were out in force, and they covered a lot of territory. I give you a sample of them and some of their vitriol.

Letters, Donald Peart, University of Sydney Music.
I, and many others, view with the greatest concern the proposal of the Federal Treasurer to increase the sales tax on musical instruments from 25 to 33 per cent.

A tax on musical instruments is a tax not only on the musical profession but on active-minded recreation, as opposed to the kind of recreation which consists in sitting still and letting oneself be amused.

It is a tax on the small, but enterprising (and therefore valuable) section of the community who like to enjoy their labour in using their minds and bodies. These will be very hard hit for the sake of an insignificant gain in revenue. They will also feel needlessly insulted by the classification of musical instruments alongside of cosmetics, jewellery, and artificial flowers as luxuries.

We are being encouraged to make an all-out effort to increase production of essential goods. Adequate recreation, such as is afforded by the playing of a musical instrument, is a necessity for such effort, as it was found by many thousands to be during the stress and anxieties of the War.

Letters, DEEWHY. Workers will not readily forget the action of the McGirr Government in sponsoring the iniquitous increases in bus and tram fares.

It is quite obvious that this represents another sell-out to pressure groups in powerful Unions. Surely the first thing to do in tackling the deficit in transport services was to look for and, if found, remove inefficiency inside the service.

Perhaps Mr McGirr would tell the travelling public how much overtime is being worked at the present moment and how many men are being paid penalty rates. Moreover, I am satisfied that in the bus I use regularly, at least 10 per cent of passengers travel free.

Letters, Mrs A Faulkner.   I cannot understand the fuss about higher tram and bus fares. These rises are only in conformity with the rising prices for other commodities of life.

I haven't seen such an enormous decline in passengers on my way to and from work. Nobody could be so foolish as to walk miles and miles to save a couple of pennies and pay absurd prices for shoe repairs.

There can only be one blessing for the higher fares. Perhaps the thousands of women and children who go to town only for window shopping, pictures, and tea-parties, will stay more often at home and leave the tram seats for the tired working people.

Letters, CUBITOR.   To many who paid heed to the Government's declaration of policy to put value back in the Pound, it is surely a matter of profound disappointment, and even anger, that more value has been taken away from the Pound by the imposition of new sales taxes of far greater amounts than the exemptions.

Many, if not most, of the items classified as "luxuries" are part-and-parcel of the average man's existence. Radio sets, suitcases, and watches are normal equipment for most people. **Cosmetics are often essential**, as a woman needs to be of reasonably attractive appearance to get and retain a job. And what parents regard photographs of their children as a luxury?

We shall continue to spend our money on such things, but with growing resentment at the unnecessarily high prices. Most of all we resent the imposition on the common **collar stud**, which has already risen in price by 1,500 per cent in ten years.

And why, of all recreational and educational media, must music (already subject to heavy import duty) be singled out for oppression, rather than beer-swilling or gardening, or **crossword puzzles**?

THE DEATH PENALTY

Over the years, one constantly recurring worry for Australian society was the death sentence. It was still occasionally practiced in this fair nation, but rarely. Some of the States had moved to get it off their statute books, and others were always thinking about it. But some people, a sizable minority, still supported it. Here is one example of the latter.

Letters, Aileen Morse. Recent reports from Australian courts cause one to wonder. To quote instances. A man found guilty of the murder of a baby, one of his acts was to stamp on it, was accorded a recommendation to mercy by the jury. On what grounds?

Another man, found guilty of strangling his wife under "extreme provocation", was sentenced to five years imprisonment. What has happened to our sense of justice? Is all the misplaced mercy to be for the slayer, because he pitches a tale of blackouts, complexes, and so on?

It is time that a murderer or two was made to pay the full penalty for his crime.

LIFE IN THE CITY

Here is a Letter that might be a bit garbled in places, but still the message gets through loud and clear.

Letters, Norman McLeod.   Do you want a decent grouch from a bushman who left your township in 1900, and has only been back for infrequent holidays since?

I have bad feet (gout) and have walked barefoot to a pillar-box every morning with a letter held plainly in my hand. My only helping friend has been a tiny girl of six or so, who asked if she could post the letter. But dozens of cars passed with blaring hoots; "get out of the road, you old cripple."

In the bush, a fellow would not need bare feet or pyjamas plainly showing under his topcoat to be hailed by every passer-by: "How far are you going, mate."

Once I tried to use a public telephone. A lady was draped over the machine and I waited for fully half an hour, tapping to show my impatience. I'm not usually rude to ladies, but could have broken my rule on this occasion.

At last, freedom to plunge and nobody waiting. But the number remained engaged and I waited, my poor feet crying for mercy. The number for "complaints" was so faint that even with the help of a "digger" friend striking matches, we failed to translate.

By courtesy of "Inquiries" we got 800, and the news gradually seeped through that something was the matter, but neither he nor I could catch on. I tried I swear for ten minutes to make the gradually rising angel voice at the other end say a plain "yes" or "no" as to whether I could get a number, but I still don't know and we left in disgust.

Don't forget that my bare, gouty toes had been suffering torture. I could not help wondering why a "plain talk" school could not be opened for our telephone lovelies so that we old fellows could be told "no" or "yes."

P.S. My address is now Carlton. I am late of Barrington Tops. But I won't be here for long, I'll swear.

Letters, Tom Boy, High School. I would appeal to matrons and all females to refrain for negative behaviour and comments about boys and men who get a crew cut.

My male friend has recently got one, and the barrage of criticism is immense. Females say he looks like a criminal, or that he looks like a boofhead in the US military forces.

For those girls who say he looks ridiculous, I point out to them that they should look at themselves. They mostly have Toni perms spoiling their good natural hair, and with their standard twin sets, walk round looking like cute little dolls. And they act like princesses.

My male friend is exactly the same as he was before he got his hair cut.

NOVEMBER NEWS ITEMS

Hollywood actor, **Peter Lawford**, flew into Melbourne. He will star in a film, *Kangaroo*, to be made here. He was greeted by **hundreds of teenage girls all saying how lovely he was**. This was **the beginning of the visits of hundreds of US stars**, and it lasted for two decades.

He was accompanied by another American actor named **Daniel Boone**, who starred in a TV series called *"Have Gun, Will Travel"*. **I am probably the only person in the world who can remember that series** when it came to Australia, but it was enormously popular....

Kangaroo, the movie, vanished without a trace. Lawford's visit had more significance because he brought with him **a short surf board,** and this then quickly replaced the long boards we had **mainly used up till then**.

Recent road statistics show that in 1949, **1,643 persons were killed on our roads** and 32,000 were injured. **This was a record toll and, on a population basis,** is much higher than the toll 70-odd years later**.

Migrant families from central Europe were being shipped in by the boatload and housed in ex-military camps round the nation. Their aim was to stay there for a few months until they could **find a new job and a new house and go their own way**....

In the meantime, the men were given lowly jobs often away from the camp for the working week. One such camp was at Cowra. In mid-November, the women threatened violence, including displaying knives, if their rations were not improved. For example, **the

government-provided ration had been four eggs a week per person. Now it was cut to one. Bread ration was halved. **Extra food was available, but it had to be bought** from the canteen or nearby shops....

It highlights the hardships that these early "Poles and Balts" faced in migrating. Language difficulties aside, they arrived with nothing, and after two years, **some of them were still in camp and still had nothing**.

The newspapers were always bashing strikers, and rarely gave them a fair go, even when their demands were fair - and **this was often the case**. And often not. **They really enjoyed sticking it to the coal miners.** But **the coal owners were not at all saintly either**....

A Basic Wage increase had recently been granted to the full labour force. It was due to start from December 4th. The miners' annual holidays were to run from December 22nd and into January. **But the owners said they would be paid at the old rate.** They called on an **obsolete arrangement** that said the holiday pay rate would be calculated on November's rate....

Whether you think it fair or not, the owners were asking for trouble. And indeed they got it, through widespread strikes. **During which the miners lost tons of wages**....

This type of **provocative action by one side followed by self-flagelation on the other**, was typical of industrial relations at the time. **No one was winning in the class battle between capitalist and labour. But one thing as certain. Automation was flowing in from England, and the miners would soon lose out to it.**

SOME KOREAN WAR EVENTS

The tragedy of Australian soldiers being killed continued. This was brought home to the nation when **the Commanding Officer of Australian troops in Korea was sadly killed**.

In terms of the battle, the front-line continued to go backwards and forwards. **General Douglas MacArthur** launched an offensive on November 24th, and said that "for all practical purposes, this should end the War, and permit the withdrawal of UN military forces. Tell the boys that when they reach the Yalu River, they are going home. I want to make good my statement that **they'll all eat Christmas dinner at home**."

Two days later, after his troops had suffered a major set-back, he said that the Chinese Communists had now officially entered the fray, and had "shattered the high hopes we had that the War could be brought to a rapid close." He pointed out that this conflict had gone from a police-keeping mission to a full international war, and called on the UN to meet and act to resolve the issue. **MacArthur, for all his bravado, was losing his god-like stature a little at this stage.**

Unfortunately, you will hear more on all this next month. But let me point out, just as one example, that **on one day**, November 12th, the US air Force dropped **10,000 bombs** on targets in North Korea. Now that's something to be really proud of.

PAYMENT TO POWs

Meanwhile, back home in Australia, far from the cries of battle, our Government had decided that a certain allowance to Australian POW's should not be paid. Here are some distressed responses.

Letters, Philip Owen, Commander, R.A.N (Ret). I write as a survivor of H.M.A.S. Perth. I was one of the last persons, if not the last person, to abandon ship.

With a Petty Officer, I cheated drowning for 12 hours through the night and some of the day by hanging on with my fingers to a piece of timber. After three days on Thrartways Island I, with about 40 other survivors, made the mainland of Java by boat. Three days later, 20 of us were captured by a particularly efficient-looking Japanese army patrol.

May I record my disgust at the reported decision of the Commonwealth Government **not to pay ex-Prisoners of War, subsistence allowance for the period of their incarceration**. As an ex-Naval officer, whose duty it was throughout 21 years of service to know and be able to interpret the Regulations, I can state that the then extant Regulation **directed the payment of three shillings per day to all persons "not fed from Service sources."**

I enjoyed this payment in comfort in the early years of the War in Alexandria. I enjoyed this comfort after the War ended, back here in Sydney in the comfort of home on shore. Why? Because I was "not victualled from Service sources."

But for three and a half years in Japan (where no one victualled me, neither my Service nor the enemy), I get nothing.

Letters, Ellis Reynolds. The Committee refusing payment of three shillings a day to ex-POW's gave as one of its reasons that the payment might, in future, weaken a soldier's will to fight. This means that they expect **some soldiers to give themselves up to the enemy so that they could get the subsistence**

allowance. Such a theory is a gratuitous insult to all citizens in Australia.

During the last world war (and in previous conflicts), Australian soldiers in battle areas lived almost continually under sub-human conditions, but to suggest that any number of them would have seriously considered changing their condition for the horror camps of the German and Italian Fascists or for the Changi and Burma railroad camps of the Japanese Fascists is simply at variance with fact.

It is to be hoped that all public bodies throughout Australia, as well as private individuals, will support the R.S.L. and other participating bodies in their demand for this just claim on behalf of former POW's.

News item, London Nov 12. Dr John Loutit, of the Medical Research Council Radiobiology Unit, announced today that it was working on a pill to make people immune to large doses of radiation that they might receive.

The pill would be administered to persons after the radiation exposure, and **assumed that the persons had survived the exposure.** Three types of chemicals were being tested, and already some chemicals were found that give partial protection.

It was not yet possible to indicate a date at which the goal of complete protection would be reached.

SQUARE-DANCING CRAZE

Otherwise sensible people were lining up to square-dance. From what I remember, for a man, you needed a weak mind, a check shirt, stupid heavy boots, a wide belt with big buckle, sometimes a broad-brimmed hat, and uncomfortable stiff pants like blue jeans. The girls also needed a weak mind, wide multi-coloured skirts, pretty white blouses, and something like bobby sox. If you had these, you could swing your partner to the left, and dosado to your heart's content.

The astute reader might get an impression that I was not all that keen on square dancing. There is some truth in that. I suppose some of my resistance was simply a by-product of the obligatory anti-American phase that teenagers were prone to. But part of it was a feeling of superiority. After all, who needed a caller out the front to tell you what to do. It was **so, so** regimented, we old-time dancers smugly said, as we went though the gay frenzy of the Pride-of-Erin.

But others thought differently. The dances swept the nation, city and country. Hundreds of thousands of people fronted up every week for years, and there were even National Championships. I did become something of a convert, and can even now allemande left with my left hand, and if necessary go sashay round my own. But really, I still prefer not to.

PUT THE REDS TO BED

Now that the Government had passed its anti-Red legislation, it was quite happy to start playing with it. But the Communist Party and nine Unions were just as happy to frustrate them. They were granted an injunction by the Full High Court, restraining the Government from prosecuting any persons or organisations **until the High Court had decided on the validity of the new law**. It did however grant permission for the police and Federal agents to raid suspected premises.

So, the nation was treated to the spectacle of all sorts of raids, particularly in Melbourne, on Union offices, and Communist offices, and any affiliated offices that happened to be in the phone book. Papers were siezed, and taken away in truck-loads. It was dramatic stuff, conducted in the full glare of the media, who were naturally determined to stir up as much public concern as possible. But, of course, no one expected such raids to yield anything. Apart from the fact that the so-called conspirators were hardly adept enough to actually conspire, if they were it could hardly be expected that they would leave their dark secrets lying round in office files.

And the silliest part of all was that they had had months knowing that the Government would soon get power to raid these offices. Can anyone imagine that these plotters to over-throw the Government in Australia would still keep their secrets in premises that were certain to be raided, just waiting for the eagle eyes of the Feds to ferret them out? Hardly likely. **It was all drama, a media circus, and calculated to impress a hopefully-gullible public with the idea that there were indeed sinister things going on.**

On November 15th the matter went to the Full Bench. Doctor Evatt was the Deputy Leader of the Labor Opposition, and he took the unusual step of appearing for the challengers. The hearing lasted into December, at which stage it was announced that a decision would be handed down in February.

To get a little ahead of myself here, I will point out that **the legislation was found by the Court to be invalid.** So Menzies had to go back to the drawing board. He did so in a remarkable way that I will cover in the next book in this series.

Comment. In each book I write, **I normally indulge myself** by pouring a bit of scorn on one topic that I cover. This year, **it was the Red-bill.** I am scornful **not** because, after a full year of extreme political manoeuvring, it had come to nothing.

Instead, I gave it the treatment because of its motivation. Mr Menzies no doubt wanted to have it passed as a possible (but dubious) means of curtailing strike action. But, I think, his main aim was to use it as a scare tactic, to worry the electorate, to make them think there was a crisis at hand, and thank god that he was there to rout the rascals. These tactics were working very well in the USA at this time, with Joe McCarthy strutting the stage.

The trouble for me is that I have seen scare tactics used time and again over the years, in many countries, both prior to and after 1950. It is like some Governments starting a war, and **wrapping themselves in the flag,** when the opportunity arises. **Such tactics always work.** And I think that it was **this** political truism that Menzies had in mind when he launched his legislation, and indeed that he was quite content to have it rejected by the High Court when it did so, because it was still a matter that he could flog in the New Year.

I am probably being a bit too cynical in saying all this, though I have a lot of evidence to support me. Still, I know that fans of Menzies can find a lot of data that makes them think he was a great man. So, after a brief period off the fence, I am now firmly back balancing on the palings, and I bid you once again to make your own decision. Still, it was good while it lasted.

THE KOREAN WAR

By the end of November, the American and UN forces had been driven back to where they started from, on the 38th parallel. All of that destruction had been for nothing, and all the deaths had been for even less. The main difference now was that the Chinese were now fully into the War, and were winning victories through their endless supply of manpower. The Americans alone, by then, had lost the lives of 5,742 men, and 27,062 were wounded, and 5,571 were missing.

Right now, they were on the run south again, and it did not augur well for the New Year.

MacArthur had just placed an embargo on news out of Korea and Japan, and so all we knew was that things were getting worse. Otherwise, the embargo would have been lifted. So, it was certain that the War would continue, and in fact it did for over two more years until, in 1953, it reached a most dramatic conclusion.

But I should tell you one vital move that affected the war **in the near future. On April 11th, 1951, President Truman sacked MacArthur.**

He said he took this step because of MacArthur's inability to give whole-hearted support to the policies of the American government. He regretted having to take this step, because MacArthur's place in history as one of the greatest commanders was fully established.

When translated, this means that McArthur was keen to extend the war up to **the Chinese border and beyond**, and Truman thought that this would lead to a **worldwide** conflict. The straw that broke the camel's back was MacArthur's **unilateral talks** proposal of a fortnight ago, and the fact that he had not cleared it with anyone. It is a fundamental concept of Western democracy that military operations **must** be subordinated to elected governments. MacArthur was challenging that principle.

Western governments in general welcomed the dismissal of the wild cannon. Our own Prime Minister had very little to say on the matter, though. The day before, he had made statements that gave MacArthur his full support, and said what a great leader he was. In any case, the war went on. The big difference was that the Reds now knew that China would not be attacked on its own soil.

A GREAT RACKET WHILE IT LASTED

On Saturday mornings in 1950, thousands of people round the nation got up early and went to their local tennis court. They watered and swept and rolled the ant-bed court, put lines on it, set the net, waited a hour for the lines to dry, and then readied themselves for a week-end of sport. Every little village or suburb in the nation had a court, and this was a ritual that was part of the nation's week.

If I look now, most of this has gone away. Most of the courts have gone, and the ant-bed is mainly synthetic grass with permanent lines, and certainly the ritual has gone.

What a pity. It was good fun.

GERMANS SETTLING IN AUSTRALIA

At the moment, Australia is warming to its task of populating this vast land by migration, and was now looking to import its new citizens from countries other than Britain.

One name that kept popping up as a source was Germany and, as soon as it did, it was howled down. Who wanted an ex-Nazi soldier as a neighbour? Would their children be so indoctrinated that they had no human decency in them? Would these children be like their forebears and hunt Jews or any one they disliked, and bash them? **Only five years after the war**, these questions sprang to mind in even the most temperate soul.

A number of writers, including Professor Julius Stone of Sydney University, reacted strongly to the suggestion.

He argued that Australia does need more young migrants. But he thought that the migration of Germans was not the answer we sought, and indeed that it would be ruinous to the nation, and could threaten our survival as a democratic nation.

He pointed out that any Germans under the age of 35 years would have been indoctrinated by a system that taught violent and aggressive nationalism, and which left them servile to any charismatic leader. Youths thus trained were intolerant to others, they persecuted Communists and other nationalities, and abhored trade unions. They were trained to hunt in packs, and at the same time, indoctrinated to accept orders, no matter how inhumane, without question.

Stone adds that "And this is not to speak of the subversion of moral standards in State-promoted sex, promiscuity, and subjection of women to German warriors, religious and racial persecution, and book-burning."

Some writers go on to argue that, since the war, attempts have been made to change the attitude of the young, but this is a hopeless task. Once a person has been indoctrinated for years in their youth, the learning has become part of them, and cannot ever be stamped out. In fact, Stone argues, their attitudes have been hardened and have increased in these belligerent youngsters.

Other persons argue that not all Germans supported Hitler. And that surely we could welcome these. The argument against this is that these people are the older Germans who could not be manipulated by Goebells and the like. **But it is not the older people that we want. It is the youth**, but we do not want tainted and bigoted and dangerous youths.

But even if we accepted some older Germans, there were **quite a lot who did support Hitler**. How could we select the ones who did not? It is an impossible task, and would leave us with supporters of Nazism who were adept at hiding their true character. Is that the type of person that we want as our neighbours?

Some of the writers went on to say that anyone, **of any age**, who actually joined the Nazi Party was committed to serve the Nazis in all aspects of their life. They absorbed and fully believed the doctrines of racial superiority, and racial inferiority. They believed in subjugation of the individual to the State, and they deplored all instruments of democracy and individuality. That means they deeply believed in credos that were foreign to all that we stood for in Australia.

Such people could never suddenly "see the light", and throw away all the convictions that had been part of them for a decade or more. All they could do was show a hypocritical face that hid their true thoughts and feelings.

Professor Stone ended his Letter with the idea that "no new aspirant to the Party could enter it unless, as a member of the Hitler Youth, he had been subjected, from the kindergarten to adulthood, to the fullest possible influence of all the poisonous Nazi doctrines.

"I hope that my fellow-citizens will join with me in emphatic disapproval of this fantastic programme of mass settlement of Nazi Party members in Australia."

The second Letter uses a different approach, but reaches the same conclusion.

Letters, M Kent Hughes, MLA. I join the Professor Julius Stone in emphatic disapproval of the proposed settlement of young ex-Nazi Party members into this our nation

In Brunswick, Germany, in 1936-7, I was teaching in a Berlitz school and had both schoolchildren and young adults as pupils, all ardent followers of Hitler. In fact, the only pupils who had not been indoctrinated beyond recall, were either Jews or older people. During my stay I made the acquaintance of many non-Nazis, but never came across the "quiescent" Nazis to whom Sir John Storey refers.

Nothing could be more dangerous to our democratic institutions than to admit young Germans, who received their education under Hitler.

Comment. The idea of large scale migration from Germany did not come to fruition, though individual families came as self-paying migrants.

I ask you a question. If you had been living in 1950 in suburbia, with good neighbours, and had been told that a German family with two small children were about to move in next to you. Suppose you knew nothing more about Germans than you had heard during the non-stop propaganda during and since the war. How would you and your neighbours have reacted?

Now let me put another few questions. Australian troops had been on Occupation duties in Japan for about four years, and a number now had brides and children from there. They were starting to trickle back here, and their families were coming also. How would your suburbia have reacted`to them? The Japanese war had been closer to home, and the Japs portrayed as completely inhuman. And the bride had no English to speak of, and a completely different culture. How would she and her children have fitted in?

The answer to the last question was that very often the adjustment was very difficult. There is a legion of stories of the hardships that these worthy families faced, and many of them ended poorly.

DECEMBER NEWS ITEMS

December 1st. No one was surprised when the Feds decided that **tobacco products and spirits were now luxuries**, and increased tax on them by about 15 per cent. Given that, I ask you to look at the tobacco brands and **see if you can remember any**....

Brands. Ardath, Champion Ruby, Havelock, Log Cabin, Black and White, Greys....

Comment. This was a period when **roll-your-own smokers were still common**. Cigarettes were rather fancy, filter tips were an innovation, and **the link with lung cancer was not suspected in Oz as yet.**

President Truman was making a lot of silly threats over Korea and the Reds. He threatened the Reds that he would drop a bomb on them somewhere. Many of his aides and his generals liked this idea....

Three newspapers in New York clubbed together to ask ten people in the street what they thought of the idea. Results included "We have to drop the bomb sooner or later. Drop one now on Korea and a second one on Moscow", " I think we should use it immediately. Look how they are behaving in the UN"...

Six of the ten were emphatic the it should be used now. The other four were more cautious only because of **the danger of retaliation....**

The US was obsessed with the so-called Red Menace, and it was about then that Senator Joe McCarthy started his highly-publicised anti-Red purge.

Three persons will be hanged in Melbourne in a few months time. One of these is **a woman of 28 years, Jean Lee** who, along with the two men, was convicted of the murder of a bookmaker....

Lee will be the first woman hanged in Victoria since the Nineteenth Century. **She was the last woman to be hanged in any part of Australia.**

Dubbo is a small country city, in NSW, and **is not renowned for its theological mastery.** But it hit the headlines in the run-up to Christmas when the **minister at the Baptist Church banned Santa Claus from his congregation.** He objects to Christmas trees on conservation grounds. He objects to Santa in the stores because some children scream when they see him....

But mainly he objects because **Santa cannot be reconciled to the teachings of Christianity,** and is in fact the patron saint of the devil. And in any case, Santa is a silly old man....

The Baptist Church stated that each Baptist church has its own freedom on such matters, and points out that **the Dubbo view is not widely held among Baptists.**

On Friday 22nd, **times were reportedly good in cities round Australia.** In Melbourne, nearly 100 women fainted in the crushes, dozens were treated by ambulances, and two died. The day was hot, and **pedestrians were jostling and pushing all day.** Pubs were full and so were the drinkers. People are taking anything. Last week, they were choosey, but not today, said one retailer. **It was indeed a record Christmas.**

HIT SONGS FROM AMERICA:

Mona Lisa	Nat King Cole
Tennessee Waltz	Patti Page
The Thing	Phil Harris
Chattanooga Shoe Shine Boy	Red Foley
Music! Music! Music!	Teresa Brewer
Cry of the Wild Goose	Frankie Lane
Goodnight Irene	Gordon Jenkins
I Can Dream, Can't I	Andrew Sisters
Beedlebum	Spike Jones
It Isn't Fair	Don Cornell
Third Man Theme	Guy Lombado
Rudolf the Red-nosed Reindeer	Gene Autry
Rag Mop	Ames Bros
Harbour Lights	Sammy Kaye
Be My Love	Mario Lanza
Ballin' the Jack	Danny Kaye
Bewitched	Doris Day
Are You Lonesome Tonight?	Al Jolson

10 MOVIES RELEASED:

All About Eve	Anne Baxter, George Saunders
Born Yesterday	Judy Holliday, William Holden
Father Of The Bride	Spencer Tracy, Elizabeth Taylor
King Solomon's Mines	Deborah Kerr, Stuart Grainger
Sunset Boulevard	William Holden, Gloria Swanson
Harvey	James Stewart, Josephine Hull
Cheaper By The Dozen	Clifton Webb, Myrna Loy
Yellow Cab Man	Red Skelton, Gloria de Haven
Treasure Island	Robert Newton, Bobby Driscoll
Tarzan and the Slavegirl	Lex Barker, Sabu

THE HOUSING INDUSTRY

Housing right throughout this land was in short supply. The construction of dwellings of all sorts was halted during the war because of a shortage of resources. On top of that, the Governments had imposed a freeze on rents that could be charged. That meant that potential landlords could see no hope of getting rents that would keep pace with inflation, and so they kept their building money in their pockets. Hence, no new housing.

After the war, the freeze on rents continued, and in fact **it continued until the middle 1960s.** So, landlords did not invest. The individual ex-digger thus had to crawl all the way to a bank manager, and jump through hoops at the same time. Then he had to go to a builder and start to build.

Everything, though, was in short supply, and every step in the process took an eternity or longer. Add to that the number of new migrants who strangely also wanted a place to sleep, and we have a housing shortage.

One consequence of this was that many new families, now with one or two children, lived with their parents. Cosy though this might be for a while, there are in fact better ways. Ex-diggers were given preference when it came to competing to rent a new property on the market, but when there were always tons of potential renters, all ex-diggers, there were always tons who missed out. Remember too that there were many good persons who did not don a uniform during the war. They also wanted somewhere to live, but because of digger-preference, they always missed out.

In brief, there were constant Letters denouncing the state of affairs. I have selected just one, who puts the case for a different approach.,

Letters, W Edwards. The building industry needs assistance from engineers, technicians, and industrial chemists who have provided a number of synthetic materials which can be cheaply produced, and which do not possess the defects of present building materials. A modern house still consists of one-third timber in spite of all defects of wearing and shrinking. There is no reason why steel should not be used for joists and rafting in fibro-constructed houses. The whole frame, including the roof, could be of fabricated steel. During the twentieth century almost all the large industries have been re-organised, but with the building industry, one of the most important in the country, the position is otherwise.

Engineering mass production methods are essential if we are to lower costs. In the Ford Willow Run Factory, huge bombers came off the line at the rate of one per hour - why can't we organise the industries of this country to produce a house per hour. It can be done if the resources were utilised to that objective.

Steps should be taken to modernise the brick and tile industries, which are 50 years behind the times. We should install modern excavators and conveyors instead of picks and shovels and trucks pushed by man-power. We smile at the Arab's plough, but our brickyards are just as ancient.

Why do builders and Government authorities **insist on building houses to last three to four generations?** Compare the motor car of today with one 20 years ago. The engineers have given us a greatly improved car at a lower cost. The chaotic state of housing will not improve until modern engineering methods of production and planning are adopted right throughout the entirety of all the building industries.

CHURCHES

During wartime, people prayed for obvious reasons. When peace came after WWII, the number of prayers offered to God and Heaven decreased as the need for comfort from a benevolent being dropped.

Added to this, though, were other considerations such as the influence of the disbelieving sciences, the doubts that many felt about the efficacy of prayers, and the feeling that the teachings from the Bible were no longer applicable in a world so advanced as the one we lived in.

There were other gripes with religion, and Letter writers provided quite a menu to select from. The messages given from the pulpit did not address the day-to-day situations that faced people. The messages of love and tolerance did not come to terms with war, the treatment of prisoners of war, forgiving Japanese, the banning of Communists, the persistence of strikes and shortages in the essentials like housing. How can people react in a world of realities, rather than an abstract world of tales from the Bible?

Then there was dissatisfaction with the clergy. Everywhere you could find clergy ready to do **fierce battle with other clergymen from different churches**. Is`this their idea of love thy neighbour? There were some churches and their clergy who seemed to have forgotten all about real religion, and who wanted only to talk about other religions and their perceived faults.

So, with these faults and others, the churches were finding it harder and harder to muster their own troops, let alone gain new adherents. Coincident with this, their influence in society in general began to diminish. Take for example, Sunday sport.

There at the start of 1950, their message was strong. Thou shalt keep holy the Sabbath Day. Yet, over the period of just one year, crowds were newly flowing through, paying their money to watch Sunday sport. Of course, the laments about this went on for years, but the practice simply kept growing and growing.

Personal Comment. For the most part, clergy do not have an easy life. They are scarcely paid, they live in old dwellings that most of us would not live in, their furnishings and appliances are from another world. When they retire, their pensions are puny. Some of them, the Catholics particularly, are forced into an unnatural world of celibacy that no normal person can live up to for life, and if they fail, they are castigated and shamed. They are separated from normal life, and called upon to perform rites and ceremonies over and over again that some must come to hate.

Still, many of them stick it out, and all I can say is hats off to them. But I must add, that the churches should have a good look at themselves and see if they can come up with a much better way. After all, I think, they can provide access, for the many, to the word of God **without all the shortcomings pointed out by writers, and all the restraints on clergy that stop them living a prosperous and happy life.**

THE WOOL LEVY

The devious minds of politicians worked right up till a few days before Christmas. At that stage, the Government got an order from a lower Court that said it was entitled to deduct, in advance, 25 per cent of the woolgrowers' cheques for next year. This is remarkable, seeing that the legality of the payment was still before the High Court, and it was by no means certain that the growers would have to pay anything at all.

Still, even though it was clearly a matter that needed resolving, it was a nice Christmas present to all concerned to know that the Government was thinking of them.

SOME CHRISTMAS PRESENTS

For Mum: Mink, fabulous mink tucked into her Christmas stocking this year! And why not, indeed. It is not, as some imagine, right out of reach. In Snows' Fur Showroom, we saw some genuine little mink scarves and ties – blue frost mink of a soft smoky colour – for as little as 16 guineas. Think of the joy it would give her to own even a small fur of precious, wonderful mink. Fourth Floor at Snows.

For little Jennie: Imagine how thrilled she will be to have her name printed in colour, at regular intervals, right along the full length of her ribbons. How important it would make her feel. It is a new idea at McCathies', and is catching on fast. They are taking orders for them up to the 21st of this month.

Each order will be ready in a week. One inch named ribbon costs two shillings a yard, one-and-a-half-inch ribbon two shillings and sixpence a yard. 199 Pitt Street.

For Grandma, maybe: Every day you will see people crowding round Ann Jacqueline's.   This may explain why....slip and panties like these, of white and pink or blue satin, bias-cut and lavishly trimmed with lace, cost only 52 shillings per set. SSW to OS. "Jeanette" pyjamas, like these of rose-sprigged heavy English Celanese, lace-trimmed in pink or blue, cost only two Pounds.

There's also a big variety of nylons, including those sheerest 15-denier, English "Aristocs" at 15 shillings. Ann Jacqueline is also well-known for her wide selection of attractive blouses and knitwear, her Jantzen, Scamp and Sutex beachwear and swimming suits.

NEWS AND VIEWS

I will close out my sections on News and Views with a few Letters on cats. I have been passing them from Chapter to Chapter since January, looking for enough space to include them. Now, a small space has appeared, and since they are of such high intellectual worth, I at last enclose them for your undoubted pleasure and wonderment.

Letters, M Hungerford. I have a tom cat, partly Persian, who lives mostly in the bush on rabbits. He comes home occasionally to be de-ticked.

I would back this cat to deal with any number of rabbits. If farmers in rabbit-infested areas had dozens of such cats - say, 50 or 100 each - the reign of the rabbits might end,

Letters, S Tapping. The idea, to introduce cats into the country to destroy rabbits was tried out on a big scale, with bitter results in 1886 and 1887.

The then-Government purchased thousands of cats in Sydney and suburbs at one shilling each, transferred them to country centres and let them loose. But instead of making any impact on the rabbits, they went semi-wild and attacked poultry and bird life, and were such a nuisance that residents had to organise shooting-parties to try to exterminate the cat pest.

You could see the remains of native birds at the foot of trees and hollow logs. Even today you can find descendants of these cats. The harm they did to our bird life is incalculable.

Letters, H McGill. The rat menace has increased alarmingly in the city area. One reason is undoubtedly the fact that the city's best rat catcher, the cat, is not allowed to carry on in sufficient numbers.

It should be made an offence to remove a cat from the city where it is doing good service by helping to exterminate an enemy of mankind.

Instead of having a healthy cat destroyed, a wiser and more humane policy would be to release it in the city where it could obtain sufficient scrappy food to strengthen it for its natural work.

PERSONAL COMMENT ON 1950

At the end of a book, in my reflective moments, I think some silly thoughts. I often throw them away next day if they seem too erratic, so if you see a blank space here you know that this time my thinking was too silly for words.

This year I have been brooding over the year 1950 itself. It is tempting to say that a year marking the half Century is a vital point, but I hope I am not that shallow. But I do think that 1950 was important, more important than most.

I say this because, to me, it marked the transition away from the war-time years to the years of liberation, if I might be so dramatic. I see the effects of the war still lingering until then, I see the rationing, and the shortages of almost everything still in place, I see the bullies in government posts still wanting forms filled in, and bank managers ruling their empires like rajahs. There were greasy hands on everything stopping progress, and there were a few million good folk who only wanted to go back to the good old pre-war days.

In 1950, the new Menzies Government came in. **This was the symbolic turning point.** The nation had rejected socialism in the elections, and that would mean that many of the war-time constraints would go. The voices of all the service personnel, who had seen other parts of the world, were ready to be heard, and so too was their refusal to live the life of subservience that their parents had known too well. It was a different population, a population that had no idea of where it was going, but was absolutely certain that it would get there. And if you look back, you can see that the nation did get there. From a nation of ice-boxes and draft horses we have grown into blistering electronics and driver-less cars.

For me, all of this progress started in 1950. A year to be remembered.

SUMMING UP 1950

It was a year of records or near-records. This was most obvious for the wool price, which just kept going higher and higher. Even in the last week before Christmas, the Brisbane Sales reached Australian records. But wheat was also at a peak, as were all commodities, courtesy of the demand created by the Korean War. As well, employment was at top levels, houses were being built, cars were being traded, people and rabbits were breeding at ever-increasing rates, and Australia was on a sporting high. For most people, this country was a pretty good place to be.

I think back to 1946, to the first book that I wrote in this series. It was a different year altogether. The heroic people who had struggled through the War were just **then** starting to blink at the light, and realise the War was really over. The nation was still racked with sadness for all the dead and wounded, yet by then some concepts of the future were starting to dominate the past. But it was everywhere a world of austerity and rationing, a world where all initiative had been seized by Governments, who were very keen to keep their hands on it.

The Labor Government was adding to this push back into the past. Ben Chifley was a staunch Socialist, and he wanted to have the State take control of some of the means of production of the nation. This had been a philosophy that was semi-popular in Europe between the Wars, and when he came to power he tried to socialise banking, and airlines, and the like. At the same time, he did his level best to keep controls on prices and costs and production of most products.

It had all changed now in 1950. Socialism had been swept away in the elections at the end of 1949. The whole feeling that there was something not patriotic about prosperity had gone away. People did not like controls and were saying so. Rationing was dead, and it was at last possible to buy cream. It was just a different place, and as I said above, it was now a pretty good place to be.

As to the future, I have had a sneak look ahead. I do not suppose I will surprise you too much if I tell you that there will be some good things ahead, and some things not so good. I will tell you as well that there are some fireworks just round the corner, in terms of the Red Bill, which you already know a little of. But also, things get pretty lively when the Government introduces compulsory military service for eighteen-year olds, and free University tuition for the bulk of Australian students. Anyway, that is next year's story, and I will leave it till then.

As for this year, I must say you have been a good audience. Actually, it is a bit hard to say that with certainty at the moment, because I have not yet finished writing the book, and have had no feedback at all. Nevertheless, I always get a bit light-headed when I am at this final stage, and I trust you will believe me when I say that you have in fact been a good audience.

More soberly, and without trying to confound the issue, let me say that 1950 for me was a good year to write about because it had so much happening, both in terms of hard news and trivia. Like 1949, which was also busy, I had to compress stories I could have written more about, and I had to leave out some gems that were worthy of reporting. But in any case, I think it has turned out to be an interesting year, and I hope you have prospered in it, and will continue to do so. May all your troubles be little ones.

COMMENTS FROM READERS

Tom Lynch, Speers Point…..Some history writers make the mistake of trying to boost their authority by including graphs and charts all over the place. You on the other hand get a much better effect by saying things like "he made a pile". Or "every one worked hours longer that they should have, and felt like death warmed up at the end of the shift." I have seen other writers waste two pages of statistics painting the same picture as you did in a few words….

Barry Marr, Adelaide….you know that I am being facetious when I say that I wish the war had gone on for years longer so that you would have written more books about it…

Edna College, Auburn…. A few times I stopped and sobbed as you brought memories of the postman delivering letters, and the dread that ordinary people felt as he neared. How you captured those feelings yet kept your coverage from becoming maudlin or bogged down is a wonder to me….

Betty Kelly. Every time you seem to be getting serious you throw in a phrase or memory that lightens up the mood. In particular, in the war when you were describing the terrible carnage of Russian troops, for no reason, you ended with a ten line description of how aggrieved you felt and ended it with "apart from that, things are pretty good here". For me, it turned the unbearable into the bearable, and I went from feeling morbid and angry back to a normal human being….

Alan Davey, Brisbane….I particularly liked the light-hearted way you described the scenes at the airports as the American high-flying entertainers flew in. I had always seen the crowd behaviour as disgraceful, but your light-hearted description of it made me realise it was in fact harmless and just good fun….

MORE INFORMATION ON THESE BOOKS

Over the past 17 years the author, Ron Williams, has written this series of books that present a social history of Australia in the post-war period. They cover the period for 1939 to 1973 with one book for each year. Thus there are 35 books.

To capture the material for each book, he worked his way through the Sydney Morning Herald and the Age/Argus day-by-day, and picked out the best stories, ideas and trivia. He then wrote them up into about 180 pages of a year-book.

He writes in a simple direct style, he has avoided statistics and charts, and has produced easily-read material that is entertaining, and instructive, and charming.

They are invaluable as gifts for birthdays, Christmas, and anniversaries, and for the oldies who are hard to buy for.

These books are available at all major retailers such as Dymocks and Collins. Also at on-line retailers such as Booktopia and Amazon, and your local newsagent.

Over the next few pages, summaries of other books in the Series are presented. A synopsis of all books in the Series is available from   boombooks.biz

****

THERE ARE 35 TITLES IN THIS SERIES

In 1948, there was no shortage of rationing and regulation, as Labor tried to convince voters that war-time restrictions should stay. Immigration Minister Calwell generously allowed five coloured immigrants from each Asian nation to settle here every year. Burials on Saturday were banned. Rowers in Oxford were given whale steak to beat meat rationing.

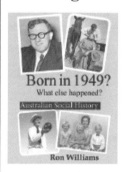

In 1949, the Reds in China could rest from their Long March, and the Reds in Australia took a battering in the pits. The rabbits ruled the paddocks, and some Churches suffered from outbreaks of dirty dancing and housie. Calwell crudely enforced the White Australia Policy, so that huge crowds on the beaches were nervous about getting a tan.

****

Chrissi and birthday books for Mum and Dad and Aunt and Uncle and cousins and family and friends and work and everyone else.

Don't forget a good read and chuckle for yourself.

In 1958, the Christian brothers bought a pub and  raffled it; some clergy thought that Christ would not be pleased. Circuses were losing animals at a great rate. Officials were in hot water because the Queen Mother wasn't given a sun shade; it didn't worry the lined-up school children, they just fainted as normal. School milk was hot news, bread home deliveries were under fire.

In 1959, Billy Graham called us to God. Perverts  are becoming gay. The Kingsgrove Slasher was getting blanket press coverage. Tea, not coffee, was still the housewife's friend. Clergy were betting against the opening of TABs. Errol, a Tasmanian devil, died. So too did Jack Davey. There are three ways to kill a snake. Aromarama is coming to your cinema.

****

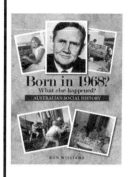

In 1968, Sydney had its teeth fluoridated, its sobriety tested for alcohol with breathalisers, and its first Kentucky Fried. And it first heart transplant. At the same time, the number of postal deliveries per day was reduced from two to one. There was still much opposition to Vietnam and demos, often violent, were everywhere all the time. The casino in Tasmania was approved.

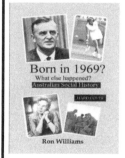

In 1969. Hollywood produced a fake movie that appeared to show a few Americans walking on the moon. The last stream train was pensioned off. There are now no Labor governments in office in all Australia. Thousands of people walked the streets in demos against the Vietnam War. The Poseidon nickel boom made the fortunes of many. Oz Magazine died an untimely death.

****

Soft covers for each of the years from 1939 to 1973.